Give him no rest

Give him no rest

Erroll Hulse

EVANGELICAL PRESS

 EVANGELICAL PRESS

Evangelical Press
Faverdale North Industrial Estate, Darlington, DL3 0PH England
email: sales@evangelicalpress.org

Evangelical Press USA
PO Box 825, Webster, NY 14580 USA
email: usa.sales@evangelicalpress.org

www.evangelicalpress.org

First published 2006

Printed in the U.S.A.

British Library Cataloguing in Publication Data available

ISBN-13 978 0 85234 283 1   ISBN 0 85234 283 7

Contents

Introduction   7

I. General Principles

1. What is revival?   17
2. Give God no rest!   35
3. Jonathan Edwards - theologian of revival   41
4. The centrality of gospel preaching in revival   53

II. Reasons for specific prayer for revival

5. The biblical doctrine of repentance demands it   73
6. The history of the church dictates it   81
7. The example of our predecessors encourages it   93
8. Our present decline compels it   105
9. The promises of Scripture urge it   119
10. Present-day revivals inspire it   133

III. Practical considerations

11. A call to prayer for revival   145

Bibliography   165
Notes   177
Index   183

Introduction — three examples of revival

This book is a call for a concert of prayer at this time, the beginning of a new millennium. In several places in the book I have included descriptions of revivals. These accounts not only endorse the reality of revival, but should also quicken in us a fervent desire to pray for a return of revival in our times. We must recognize the importance of prayer. Most revivals have their genesis in prayer meetings — sometimes the conventional weekly church prayer meeting, sometimes children praying in schools, and sometimes students praying in colleges. There are many examples, but by way of introduction I will refer to three.

I take as my first choice the 1858 revival in America. My principal reason for choosing this particular revival is that it was characterized by its evident inception in prayer meetings and illustrates the concept of a concert of prayer for revival. It consisted of a great national spiritual awakening which very clearly had its genesis in prayer meetings.

Dr Edwin Orr, a famous twentieth-century historian, devoted his life to researching and chronicling revivals. Towards the end of his life he came to the conclusion that 'the Awakening of 1857-58 was the most thorough and most wholesome ever known in the Christian Church'.[1] Edwin Orr wrote:

> The influence of the awakening was felt everywhere in the nation. It first moved in the great cities, but it also spread through every town and village and country

hamlet, swamping school and college. It affected all classes without respect to their condition. A divine influence seemed to pervade the land, and men's hearts were strangely warmed by a Power that was outpoured in unusual ways. There was no fanaticism. There was remarkable unanimity of approval among religious and secular observers alike, with scarcely one critical voice heard anywhere. It seemed to many that the fruits of Pentecost had been repeated a thousand-fold. At any rate the number of conversions reported soon reached the total of 50,000 weekly, a figure borne out by church statistics showing an average of 10,000 additions to church membership a week for a period of two years.[2]

The beginning of the revival in New York is traced to a small prayer meeting begun by Jeremiah Lanphier. However, the excellent historian Roy J. Fish documents the fact that revival had begun in other parts of America. James W. Alexander was of the opinion that the revival had already started.[3] Yet there is no doubt that New York as a city was the most prominent centre of the revival that spread right across the continent and to other parts of the world.

Jeremiah Calvin Lanphier, born in 1809 and converted in 1842, was appointed in July 1857 to be an inner city missionary in New York and was employed by the Dutch Reformed Church situated on Fulton Street. As he sought to evangelize in hotels, boarding houses and business establishments, he encouraged himself in prayer. The thought came to him that it would be good to have a prayer meeting at midday to which business men might come and go as they were able. He had some invitations printed to that effect and advertised the fact that at noon on 23 September a room would be available on the third floor at the back of the North Dutch Church on Fulton Street. These invitations were liberally distributed in hotels, factories and businesses as well as to private residences in the neighbourhood.

At the appointed time Mr Lanphier was the only one present. For the next thirty minutes no one came, but then one by one men arrived to make a total of six persons present.

A week later twenty attended the meeting and the week after that the number doubled to forty at which gathering the suggestion was made that the prayer meeting should become a daily event. This was agreed upon and in the days which followed there was a steady increase in attendance.

Within six months ten thousand businessmen were gathering daily for prayer in New York in about 150 different groups. It was evident that the revival had begun with the Holy Spirit being poured out along the lines of Zechariah 12:10: 'And I will pour out on the house of David and the inhabitants of Jerusalem a spirit of grace and supplication.' Orr notes, 'Undoubtedly the greatest revival in New York's colourful history was sweeping the city, and it was of such a nature as to make the whole nation curious.'[4] Early it was seen that many were under conviction of sin, seeking an interest in Christ and enquiring what they should do to be saved.[5]

What took place in this spiritual awakening resembled in nature the waters described by Ezekiel: a gradual increase, first ankle deep, then up to the waist, and then waters to swim in (Ezek. 47). All kinds of people began to attend — professional men, merchants, clerks, butchers, bakers, and labourers, men from every walk of life. At first those who came were only men but gradually women also began to attend. By mid January the numbers had increased to the point where all three lecture rooms were filled to overflowing with different men leading the meetings in each. The format was flexible. Hymns were sung and portions of Scripture were read. Prayers were required to be brief to allow for participation.

One of the first cities affected was Philadelphia. A prayer meeting was begun there in November 1857 but at first it was small and did not exceed thirty-six in attendance. But then in February 1858 the venue was moved and gradually the numbers attending increased to over 2,500.[6]

In Chicago 2,000 and upwards daily attended the Metropolitan Theatre for a prayer meeting. Prayer meetings multiplied throughout the city of Boston. Not only did the great cities feel the throbbings of this mighty revival, but also there was scarcely a town or village throughout the Northern States that was not visited with showers of refreshing grace.

The presence of God seemed to pervade the land. The minds of men were wonderfully moved and their hearts softened.[7]

The following year a great revival resembling in many ways the one in America came to parts of Britain. The Banner of Truth recently republished a thrilling account of the 1859 Welsh revival.[8]

This revival in America was characterized from the beginning by noonday prayer meetings but was by no means confined to that. Of course, the regular preaching was there. Extra preaching services were organized as they were needed.

At the end of the day the only satisfactory way to establish the nature and extent of revivals is to read the eye witness reports published at the time. That involves much hard work. The Presbyterian Magazine describes the extent of the revival as follows:

> A remarkable feature in the present religious movement is the great extent of the work. It is not confined to a single sector of the country, not to a single Christian denomination; but with few exceptions, it extends to all. From the Atlantic to the Pacific Ocean there is not a territory in which the gracious steppings of Jehovah have not been more or less visible.
>
> If any one great centre can be designated as the radiant point from which the mighty movement has proceeded it is the principal commercial metropolis of the United States, the city of New York. But the work has been so nearly simultaneous in different places as to indicate the influence of the Holy Spirit.[9]

This witness goes on to suggest that the character of the work was more like rain falling evenly over the land than irrigation whereby water is channelled from one source. He goes on to say, 'all evangelical churches have enjoyed in common this merciful visitation, coming like showers from heaven direct from the throne of God'.[10] He also notes that Jews were affected as well as Gentiles. The revival affected people of diverse occupations and cultures, including fishermen (especially at a place called Rockaway), college students, and Native Americans.

John L. Girardeau of South Carolina described the revival as the greatest event of his life. Girardeau's life is recorded in a superb book authored by Douglas Kelly and published in 1992 by the Banner of Truth. Kelly provides fascinating biographies of four illustrious preachers in the South: Daniel Baker, James Henley Thornwell, Benjamin Morgan Palmer and John L. Girardeau. Girardeau was a preacher of extraordinary spiritual unction who devoted the first part of his life to preaching and pastoring among the black slave community. He had a congregation of about 1,500 which had about ninety percent black and ten percent white members. After the civil war (1851-1865) Girardeau was called to the work of training men for the ministry in Columbia Theological Seminary. But regarding the revival, it began in the late fifties with a prayer meeting that constantly increased until the house was filled. Some of the officers of the church wanted Girardeau to commence preaching services, but he steadily refused, waiting for the outpouring of the Spirit. His view was that the Father had given to Jesus, as the King and Head of the church, the gift of the Holy Spirit, and that Jesus in his sovereign administration of the affairs of his church, bestowed him upon whatsoever he pleased, and in whatever measure he pleased. Day after day he, therefore, kept his prayer addressed directly to the mediatorial throne for the Holy Spirit to come in mighty reviving power.

One evening while leading the people in prayer, he received a sensation as if a bolt of electricity had struck his head and diffused itself through his whole body. For a little while he stood speechless under the strange physical feeling. Then he said: 'The Holy Spirit has come; we will begin preaching tomorrow evening.' He closed the service with a hymn, dismissed the congregation, and came down from the pulpit; but no one left the house. The whole congregation had quietly resumed its seat. Instantly he realized the situation. The Holy Spirit had not only come to him — he had also taken possession of the hearts of the people. Immediately he began exhorting them to accept the gospel. They began to sob softly, like the falling of rain; then, with deeper emotion, to weep bitterly, or to rejoice loudly, according to their circumstances. It was midnight before he could dismiss his congregation. A noted evangelist from the North who was present said, between his sobs, to an officer of the church: 'I never saw it on this fashion!' The meeting went on night and day for eight weeks. Large numbers of both black and white were converted and joined the various churches of the city. Girardeau's church was wonderfully built up. He was accustomed to say that he could always count on those who were converted in that meeting. This was probably due to the deep work of conviction of sin, the protracted period of deep conviction, the clear sense of pardon, and the joyful witness of the Spirit to their adoption.

His sermons during the meetings, as shown by his notes, were very instructive. He dealt with the great doctrines of sin, regeneration, faith, justification, repentance and other subjects. None of those who went through these meetings ever forgot the wonderful preaching.

About this period revivals occurred over almost the whole country and large numbers of young men were brought into the church. Dr Girardeau frequently referred to this as the Lord's mercy in gathering his elect for the great war was soon to sweep so many of them into eternity.[11]

My second example compared to the previous description is very brief. A powerful revival took place in Northern Ireland in 1859. This revival illustrates that a great work can have a tiny beginning.

In 1856 in Ballemena a certain Mrs Colville influenced a young man, James McQuilkin, to conversion. He in turn led three of his friends to Christ. The four of them agreed to meet every week for prayer and Bible study. They chose an old schoolhouse and during the winter of 1857 and 1858 kept themselves warm with armfuls of peat gathered on the way to the schoolhouse every Friday evening. While the peat warmed their bodies, the Spirit kindled the fire in their hearts. Two more joined them, including an old man named Marshall. By the end of 1858 the number of participants at the prayer meeting had grown to fifty. Intercession without distraction to other subjects was made for an outpouring of the Holy Spirit on themselves and the country. These prayers and possibly many others (for only the Great Day will declare all) were wonderfully answered in 1859 when, it is estimated, 100,000 were converted in Ulster.[12]

My third illustration centres in South Africa at the beginning of the twentieth century. This revival began towards the end of the Boer War (1899-1902). To prevent recurring escapes, the British deported the captured Boer soldiers to Ceylon, now called Sri Lanka. 5,000 prisoners of war were confined in a camp there. These men were very discouraged by their sufferings, by bereavements and by anxiety over the loss of their homes, many of which had been burned down. One night two brothers fell to quarrelling. The chaplain (domine) exhorted them to go out to the rugby field that the prisoners had made for themselves, and there pray about their problem rather than quarrel about it. They took his advice. Later they came back to report that the Holy Spirit had fallen upon them while they were at prayer. They urged others to accompany them to the same place the next evening. This was done and the Holy Spirit again fell upon the men who gathered for prayer. A revival had broken out. The prayer meeting became a fixed event and led to 2,000 out of 5,000 prisoners of war professing faith in Christ.

These accounts have been selected because they illustrate prayer as the genesis of revival. With regards to the account of the spiritual awakening in Sri Lanka, it is remarkable to discover that similar powerful visitations of the Holy Spirit came to the South African Boer prisoners who had been transported to St Helena, Bermuda and India. Amazing awakening took place among the prisoners in Bermuda. In India, where 1,000 men were detained behind thick walls and barbed wire, a group of men met daily for prayer until a powerful visitation ensued. There was an extraordinary increase of zeal for missionary service and following the war 200 men were trained and sent to mission fields. Compare that to the feeble state of missionary zeal among us today! 1905 was a time of revival in South Africa with remarkable outpourings of the Holy Spirit. Beginning with the Dutch Reformed Church at Villiersdorp, awakening spread to many other congregations. In each case the news of God's power and grace created a burden for prayer which in turn led to further spiritual awakening.[13]

It is my earnest hope that accounts like these will sustain interest and also inspire readers to take this subject more seriously.

General Principles

1. What is revival?

We need to preserve a very clear view of what genuine revival is and in so doing appreciate afresh just how marvellous such a work of grace is. Those who have themselves witnessed the power of the Holy Spirit in revival hardly need written descriptions and definitions to help them. However, those who have never known the reality of revival are more prone to settle for something less.

Some believe that revival is linked to the restoration of supernatural gifts to the church. An example of this is Edward Irving (1792-1828). His life is wonderfully described in a biography by Arnold Dallimore and published by the Banner of Truth. Those who followed Irving started an apostolic denomination with apostles. The same idea is pursued by the contemporary denomination known as New Frontiers which has emerged since the 1970s. The cessation of apostles and apostolic signs, miracles and wonders was upheld by Jonathan Edwards and is expounded in his book *Charity and Its Fruits*, published by the Banner of Truth. The major revivals of the past have indeed been noted for phenomena, but these have not been of the kind seen in the modern charismatic movement. A deep conviction of sin and repentance is the main mark of true revival rather than the high emotions, sensations and excitement that are created by manipulation.

It is imperative that we preserve the true meaning of the words 'revival' and 'awakening' and also examine other terms which are sometimes used, such as 'renewal' and 'divine visitation'. The complexity of the subject can be appreciated when we realize that it is not just a matter of defining clear categories. One category can merge into another. For the sake of analysis theologians divide man into parts: affections, intellect, will, conscience and body, but we all know that man is essentially one. The same principle applies when we attempt to analyse the work of God in revival. Nevertheless the value of defining what we mean should become clearer as we proceed.

What is revival?

At the Puritan Conference in London in 1959, Dr Martyn Lloyd-Jones gave a historical and theological survey of revival. He followed the standard definition of revival, but expressed it in his usual gripping way:

> It is an experience in the life of the Church when the Holy Spirit does an unusual work. He does that work, primarily, amongst the members of the Church; it is a reviving of the believers. You cannot revive something that has never had life, so revival, by definition, is first of all an enlivening and quickening and awakening of lethargic, sleeping, almost moribund Church members. Suddenly the power of the Spirit comes upon them and they are brought into a new and more profound awareness of the truths that they had previously held intellectually, and perhaps at a deeper level too. They are humbled, they are convicted of sin, they are terrified at themselves. Many of them feel that they have never been Christians. And they come to see the great salvation of God in all its glory and to feel its power. Then, as the result of their quickening and enlivening, they begin to pray. New power comes into the preaching of the ministers, and the result of this is that large numbers who were previously outside the Church are converted and brought in. So the two main characteristics of revival are, first, this extraordinary enlivening of the members of the Church, and second, the conversion of masses of people who hitherto have been outside in indifference and sin. (There are many other consequences which I do not stay to mention, such as the needful provision of larger church buildings, establishing of new causes, large numbers of men offering themselves for the ministry and beginning to train, and so

on.) Here then, in essence, is a definition of what we mean by revival.[1]

Revival and awakening

In his book on the Holy Spirit, James Buchanan defines revival in the same way as Dr Martyn Lloyd-Jones in the passage just quoted. He writes:

> Revival properly consists in two things: a general importation of new life, vigour and power to those who are already of the number of God's people; and a remarkable awakening and conversion of souls who have hitherto been careless and unbelieving; in other words it consists in a new spiritual life imparted to the dead, and a new spiritual life imparted to the living.[2]

Edwin Orr, who devoted most of his ministry to documenting revivals, suggested an important distinction between the way we use the words 'revival' and 'awakening'. He suggested that 'revival' is something which properly affects the churches. It produces deep repentance and greater holiness, with a new release of power in witness and evangelism. 'Awakening', however, refers primarily to the conversion of unbelievers, who are 'awakened' from spiritual death and brought to life in Christ.

Another way of drawing this distinction would be to refer to 'vival', in contrast to revival. In the book of Acts large numbers of converts are reported at places like Derbe, Thessalonica, Corinth and Ephesus. It would be more accurate to describe this as 'vival', since it was life for the first time. By contrast, the revivals of the eighteenth and nineteenth centuries, or the revival in Wales in 1904, represented the reviving of existing churches, with a subsequent great increase of converts. Strictly speaking, the revival among the Indians under the ministry of David Brainerd was 'vival', spiritual life for the first time. Wycliffe Bible translators and other pioneer missionaries labouring in unevangelized fields report harvests of souls in many different areas of the world. This harvesting is suitably described as 'vival'. To cite an example, a friend wrote to me saying that he had visited East Timor (now the independent state of Timor Lorosae) in 1964. Then there were six known believers. Today the largest denomination there is the Assemblies of God with 12,000 members. Another example is Nepal. No Christian was officially allowed to live in Nepal before 1960. By 1990 there was a measure of religious freedom but not to evangelize. The first group of twenty-nine believers was formed in 1959. By 1985 it is estimated that there were 50,000 believers and in spite of much persecution the number had increased to 200,000 by 1990. By 2000 the estimate was between 400,000 and 500,000 in 3,000 congregations.[3]

Essential characteristics of a revival

Pentecost was the first revival in the new covenant age and it was also 'vival', the first bursting forth of spiritual life under the dominion of the resurrected Christ. Four basic characteristics of Pentecost characterize all revivals of this epoch. We shall examine each of these in turn.

1. The sense of God's nearness and especially an awareness of his holiness and majesty

This first feature is vital. It consists of what is sometimes referred to as the 'Shekinah glory' of God's presence. In Exodus 40:34 and 2 Chronicles 7:1 we read of the cloud of the Lord's presence filling the tabernacle and the glory of the Lord filling the temple. There may not be any visible cloud, but in all true revival the presence of the Lord is sensed in an awesome way.

This phenomenon is important because it focuses on the fact that revival is God coming down on mankind, with the result that they are humbled. There are religious movements in Africa which involve huge numbers of people who sing in a very impressive way. These movements, known as Zionist movements, are often heterodox in doctrine. Sometimes the singing is of a very high order, far above the standard which we are used to in Europe. One can easily get the impression that a great revival is in progress. But

it is always essential for us to use our minds and analyse what is
going on (Rom. 12:1, 2). Some consider such questioning to be
sinful, but it is not. I do not mean that we should be censorious;
it is rather that we are duty bound to test everything by Scripture.
When there is great emotion we need to ask ourselves about the
source of that feeling. Is it something that has been worked up
by manipulators who are experts in controlling crowds, or is it
something which is from heaven? Is there glorying in man, or is
the focus on the glory of the triune God? Is there a glorying in
patriotism, or nationalism, or tribalism? Often religion is used as
a veneer to cover what is, in essence, idolatry.

Often the charismatic movement is characterized by a strong
emphasis on the emotions. In mass meetings there is sometimes
a deliberate method used to bring great crowds to a high point
of excitement and exuberance. This is emotion worked up from
within, whereas revival is the Holy Spirit coming down. When
he comes down there is a prostrating effect; the awesomeness
and glory of God's holiness are felt in an overwhelming way.
We see this illustrated in the personal experience of the patriarch
Jacob when the Lord met with him at Bethel. Jacob's response
was expressed in these words: 'How awesome is this place! This
is none other than the house of God; this is the gate of heaven'
(Gen. 28:17).

An awareness of the nearness of God is the chief characteristic
of all true revivals (Ps. 80; Isa. 64; John 14:17; 1 Cor. 14:24-25).
The expression, 'I will live among you', conveys the idea of this
nearness. '"Shout and be glad, O Daughter of Zion. For I am coming, and I will live among you," declares the Lord. "Many nations
will be joined with the Lord in that day and will become my people.
I will live among you"' (Zech. 2:10-11). This nearness is characteristic of the next world: 'Now the dwelling of God is with men, and
he will live with them. They will be his people, and God himself will
be with them and be their God' (Rev. 21:3).

At Pentecost everyone was filled with awe (Acts 2:43). A re-
alization of the holiness of God is also one of the hallmarks of
revival. The initial experience of fear of God and conviction of sin
is followed by intense joy and love: 'They broke bread in their

homes and ate together with glad and sincere hearts, praising God and enjoying the favor of all the people. And the Lord added to their number daily those who were being saved' (Acts 2:46-47).

In 1735 a remarkable revival came to the village of North-ampton and villages in Connecticut. Jonathan Edwards who was to become famous through his book, *A Narrative of Surprising Conversions*, described this revival by drawing attention to the phenomena of the felt sense of the presence of God. Edwards writes:

> Presently upon this, a great and earnest concern about the great things of religion, and the eternal world, became universal in all parts of the town, and among persons of all degrees, and all ages. The engagedness of their hearts in this great concern could not be hid; it appeared in their very countenances. It then was a dreadful thing amongst us to lie out of Christ, in danger every day of dropping into hell.[4]

This sense of the fear of God is a vital element of true revival. It is the feature which is missing from contemporary evangelicalism. It is of such importance that we should look at it in more detail as it applies to revivals.

Edward Payson, who ministered at Portland, Maine, USA (1807-1827), describes the way in which the Holy Spirit works through preaching in a revival:

> Large congregations often sit and hear a message from God, while perhaps not a single individual among them feels that the message is addressed to himself, or that he has any personal concern in it. But it is not so when God speaks with his still small voice. Everyone, to whom God thus speaks, feels that he is spoken to, and that he is called, as it were, by name. Hence while multitudes are around him, he sits as it were alone. At him alone the preacher seems to aim. On him alone his eye seems to be fixed. To him alone every word seems to come. Absorbed in the truths thus presented, in reflecting on his own conduct,

guilt, and danger, and on the character and commands of God, he is almost unconscious of the presence of his fellow worshippers; his attention is chained to the subject by bonds which he cannot break, and sentence after sentence, truth after truth, falls upon his ear, and is impressed on his conscience with a weight, an energy, and an efficacy, which omnipotence alone can give. Sent email to try to find source... author doesn't know.

And when God thus speaks to the whole or the greatest part of an assembly at once, as he sometimes does, when he comes to revive his work extensively, these effects are experienced, and these appearances exhibited by all. No scene, on this side the bar of God, can be more awfully, overpoweringly solemn, than the scene which such an assembly exhibits. Then the Father of spirits is present to the spirits he has made; present to each of them, and speaking to each. Each one feels that the eye of God is upon him, that the voice of God is speaking to him. Each one, therefore, though surrounded by numbers, mourns solitary and apart. The powers of the world to come are felt. Eternity, with all its crushing realities, opens to view, and descends upon the mind. The final sentence, though uttered by human lips, comes with scarcely less weight, than if pronounced by the Judge himself. All countenances gather blackness, and a stillness, solemn, profound, and awful, pervades the place, interrupted only by a stifled sob, or a half-repressed sigh. My hearers, such scenes have been witnessed. Within a very few years they have been witnessed in hundreds of places.[5]

2. A greatly intensified work of the Holy Spirit in conviction of sin and giving repentance and faith

The second essential characteristic of genuine revival points us to the work of the Holy Spirit in regeneration.

This is illustrated by the description given by Edwards of the revival in Northampton in 1735:

There was scarcely a single person in the town, old or young, left unconcerned about the great things of the eternal world. Those who were wont to be the vainest and loosest, and those who had been most disposed to think and speak slightly of vital and experimental religion, were now generally subject to great awakenings. And the work of conversion was carried on in a most astonishing manner, and increased more and more; souls did as it were by flocks come to Jesus Christ.[6]

Yet by no means do all who in times of revival profess to have faith and repentance prove to be genuine. Time alone proves whether they are or not. Satan seeks to counterfeit revival and he is very active in genuine revivals to sow false seeds and promote false professions. Having witnessed revival, first in his own church in 1735 and then later on a wider scale in the Great Awakening of 1740, Jonathan Edwards realized the need to provide principles by which we can distinguish the true from the false. He wrote two crucial works on this theme: the first, a short work, was called *The Distinguishing Marks of a Work of the Spirit of God,* and the second, a much fuller and more detailed book, was entitled, *The Religious Affections.* The latter, which is regarded as his best work and the most profound book ever written on the subject, is really an enlargement of the first. Edwards proceeds in a straightforward way to describe what are not signs of true revival and then goes on to show what are the signs which characterize a true work of God.

In brief, Edwards shows that none of the following are true signs of a work of God: great emotions, great effects on the body (such as tears, groans, loud cries, agonies or prostrations), an appearance of love, joy or great excitement, much time and zeal spent in duty, great expressions of praise or moving testimonies. Edwards observed that people can exhibit all kinds of emotions and yet fall away after the revival. So what then are the true signs?

A true sign of a work of God is a delight in the excellency of God, his holy character and his truth. This arises from an illumination of the Holy Spirit. 'Holy affections are not heat without light; but evermore arise from the information of the understanding, some spiritual instruction which the mind receives, some light or actual knowledge. The child of God is graciously affected because he sees and understands something more of divine things than he did before, more of God or Christ, and of the glorious things exhibited in the gospel'.[7] True religious affections are attended by what Edwards calls 'evangelical humiliation'. The believer has a sense of his own utter insufficiency and the hateful nature of his own sin, from which he turns, coming to depend on God's provision of righteousness. One of the true signs is a change of nature, the new birth, and the creation of a new disposition which has the likeness of Jesus and is characterized by a beautiful symmetry and proportion. A vital sign is fruit in Christian practice.

3. A marvellous increase in the numbers added to the church

In the Great Awakening in 1740-42 it is reckoned that 50,000 were added to the churches of New England, and about 300,000 across all thirteen colonies. In what we now call the 'forgotten revival' between the years 1790 and 1840, one and a half million people were gathered into chapels in England and Wales alone. That constituted one out of every ten people in the country being converted and brought into the nonconformist chapels. In the revival in 1859 around 100,000 were added to the churches in Ulster and 50,000 to the churches in Wales. It is estimated that in the 1859 revival in the USA over two million were added to the churches.

Revivals are times of God's personal intervention in great power. Revivals differ in character, yet they always have the three characteristics described here. True revivals have a powerful effect on society as a whole in turning back the tide of immorality and vice. True revivals are bad news for breweries, distillers and the gambling industry. True revivals will bring down the divorce rate and heighten society's view of the sanctity of life.

In April 1937, after nine years of work, missionaries to Ethiopia were compelled to leave that country. There were only forty-eight known indigenous believers. In 1943, after a cruel occupation by the Italians, the missionaries returned to find that about 100 churches had sprung up, representing 10,000 believers. An awakening has ensued in Ethiopia (population sixty-two million) which has resulted in an increase from 240,000 adherents in 1950 to about eleven million in the year 2000.

Mizoram (860,000) and Nagaland (1,600,000) are two small states in North Eastern India. Revivals were recorded in Nagaland in 1956, 1966 and 1972. Nagaland represents the highest percentage (sixty percent) of Baptists in any state in the world. Thousands of Nagas serve the Lord in other parts of India. Likewise in Mizoram revivals have transformed society and it is now regarded as the most literate and well-educated state of India. Mizoram is one of the most active Christians states in the world. Needless to say, all statistics are subject to debate and the depth of a work can only be assessed by visiting the countries concerned. Whatever reservations we may express, it is undeniable that a very great change has taken place in these places in a short space of time.

The impact made on any nation in a revival is great. But we can also view the marvellous increase in more local terms. A revival in the city of Boston, USA, from September 1841 to September 1842 saw all the churches affected, with about a sixty percent increase in membership of the Baptist, Congregational and Methodist churches, and a smaller increase of fifteen percent in the Episcopal churches. One Baptist church increased in membership from 161 to 287 during that time.

4. Powerful preaching of the gospel

The primacy of preaching in revival is seen in the book of Acts. I have devoted chapter four to this theme. Writing on the subject of 'Powerful Preaching', Geoffrey Thomas has this to say:

> One of the great perils that face preachers of the Reformed faith is the problem of a hyper-intellectualism, that is, the constant danger of lapsing into a purely cerebral form of proclamation, which falls exclusively on the intellect. Men become obsessed with doctrine and end up as brain-oriented preachers. There is consequently a fearful impoverishment in their hearers emotionally, devotionally and practically. Such pastors are men of books and not men of

people; they know the doctrines, but they know nothing of the emotional side of religion. They set little store upon experience or upon constant fellowship and interaction with almighty God ... The problem is universal. There is not a denomination or fellowship of pastors that does not designate powerlessness in the pulpit as its greatest weakness, and there is no shortage of homiletic literature that suggests to preachers the source of power and a revolution to their ministry. For some the answer is glossolalia, but the powerlessness is evident in Pentecostal pulpits as in non-Pentecostal. For others the answer is intimidatingly austere and almost frighteningly monastic in its tone — agonizing in prayer, fasting, mortification, and self-denial are all absolutized as the only answer to our powerlessness. How it intimidates the young pastor![8]

Where is power for preaching to be found? The only way of power suggested in the New Testament is with the Holy Spirit sent down from heaven (1 Thess. 1:4-5). That is unlikely to be our experience if we misrepresent what the Holy Spirit has inspired in the Word of God by faulty exegesis and shoddy expository workmanship. The apostles summed up the dual needs of prayer and hard study when they explained the necessity of the appointment of deacons: 'It would not be right for us to neglect the ministry of the word of God in order to wait on tables ... We will give our attention to prayer and the ministry of the word'(Acts 6:2).

It is easy to forget that the power lies in the Word of God. But 'the word of God is living and active' (Heb. 4:12). Paul exhorted Timothy, 'Preach the Word' (2 Tim. 4:2). This is so basic, yet it seems that many ministers cease to believe that preaching the gospel in the expository way is 'the power of God' (Rom.1:16). They direct their principal energies to activities of all kinds, to the neglect of study combined with prayerful meditation. 'The preacher and piety' forms the subject of a twenty-eight page exposition in the book with the title *Preaching*.[9] The life of piety is vital, combined with evangelistic enterprise and constant work in God's Word. It is as we continue fervently in that way that we intercede for, and look for, revival today.

A consideration of the term 'renewal'

It is helpful to consider this expression which has been used increasingly in recent years. We hear of 'ecumenical renewal', 'li-
turgical renewal', 'charismatic renewal' and 'theological or doctrinal renewal'. The most common reference today is to charismatic renewal, which is difficult to assess since it varies so much
in character. It can mean an emotional religious extravaganza, or
it can mean impressive mass choirs accompanied by thunderous
preaching.

Charismatic renewal has often brought positive results. At its
best it has achieved an evangelical impact on hitherto spiritually
lifeless liberal, Anglo-Catholic, or Roman Catholic churches. Even
though these charismatic renewals may fall far short of what we
would desire from a theological point of view, they are significant
because many have been turned from a sacramental mentality
to a Bible-centred outlook. That this renewal has not proceeded
further to reformation may well be due to a lack of leadership. The
great sixteenth-century Reformation was characterized by leaders
of tremendous ability in the Scriptures.

In the 1960s and 1970s a theological renewal took place in
Britain. Many evangelicals embraced the doctrines of grace. It is
not by human agency or by human persuasion, but by the power
of the Holy Spirit that we come to understand and appreciate sovereign grace. All the learning and all the books in the world cannot
persuade anyone of the sovereignty of God. Such a persuasion
in the heart is the work of the Spirit. This doctrinal renewal was
Puritan in that it included the practical and devotional emphases
of the Puritan tradition. It was a movement associated with the re-
publication of Reformed and Puritan books by the Banner of Truth
Trust. It was not merely an intellectual renewal, but it also had the
most powerful effects upon the lives of many believers. Christians
who were powerfully renewed at that time have subsequently not
deviated from their doctrinal and devotional convictions and some
have exercised fruitful ministries in many nations.

The word 'renewal' serves then, as a term which describes
a change and improvement, but which falls short of what we
understand as revival.[10]

What is meant by 'a divine visitation'?

There are many instances in which the word 'revival' is not used because the events described may be limited in power or extent. The late Walter Brehaut (1890-1972) of Guernsey was involved in a time of special blessing among fishermen in one part of the island in 1923-24. The way in which the men were converted was extraordinary — some in their beds at night and others as they walked along the road. Perhaps that movement of the Holy Spirit is better called a 'divine visitation' since the work was confined to one segment of society.

The word 'visitation' sounds old-fashioned. Where does it originate? Jeremiah might supply the answer because he complained that the Saviour of Israel was like a wayfaring man or traveller through a country, who stays at a hotel for only one night. The Saviour was like someone who made only fleeting visits. Yet just as a brilliant physician can do much good in only a few hours of surgery, so the great Physician of souls can accomplish in one visit what we could not accomplish in a lifetime.

When it is wise to do so, and providing we give all the glory to God, to report times of refreshing can be encouraging to others. We live in a barren time but have not been left destitute. I know of a preacher in Eastern Europe who experienced a divine visitation in a preaching service. Fourteen were converted during the sermon. Six months later the converts, having proved themselves, were baptized. I have been privileged to witness the power of God at work in a divine visitation. In one night a whole group of young people were powerfully and lastingly converted while they were in different prayer groups.

A contemporary minister testifies that his church in Suffolk has known two powerful divine visitations, one in the late 1970s and one in 1985. Conversions took place in a powerful way characteristic of revival, but those experiences were strictly confined to one place and so the term 'revival' should not be used. Such visitations, however, are tokens of the Lord's presence, and serve as encouragements to pray earnestly that he will come, not as a wayfaring traveller, but to stay with us in revival power.

In the year 1931, 135 were added to the membership of the church at Sandfields, Aberavon, in Wales, where Dr Martyn Lloyd-Jones was the minister. Aged thirty-one, Dr Lloyd-Jones had not long been in the ministry. One hundred and twenty-eight of the 135 were 'from the world'.[11] The previous year had seen an increase of eighty-eight of whom seventy were 'from the world'. Strictly speaking, it is better to describe a local revival as a visitation. Clearly the usage of terms is not going to change easily but the advantages of correct terminology should be obvious.

The false 'transformations movement'

Having described the terms that are used to describe progress in the churches, it is important to warn against a dangerous movement that uses the revivalistic title 'transformations'.

The 'Transformations Revival' is championed by George Otis and Peter Wagner is a dispensationally ill-conceived attempt to uproot the kingdom of darkness and visibly establish the kingdom of God on earth.

This false revival based on Peter Wagner and George Otis conceptualizes spiritual mapping and spiritual warfare. The video, *Transformations*, by George Otis, has been widely distributed, recommended and shown throughout South Africa to introduce people to an unbiblical type of spiritual warfare.

The seduction of this Christianity is often very subtle. This movement counterfeits revival. Jesus is still preached by these spiritual leaders, but the message of the Cross is not central to their preaching. Through a reinterpretation of the meaning and significance of the Cross, Jesus is changed into another Jesus. The heart of the gospel message is twisted so that the emphasis on sin and the inherent sinful nature of man is shifted to the sin of the community, the city, or nations that are ruled by Satan. The solution to this problem is not personal regeneration but spiritual warfare enforced by a united, ecumenical Christendom against the kingdom of Satan. It is evident that another spirit is manifested during such meetings. It is the spirit of the 'angel of light', who gives new revelations and new interpretations of the Bible, resulting in a wrong concept of revival. It proceeds on the basis of unity at all costs, that is, unity without reference to doctrinal foundations. It proceeds too along the lines of feeling especially during mass rallies where emotions are stirred and a warm, corporate feeling of love binds people together. These experiences are not grounded in Scripture. People are not convicted of personal sin and unrighteousness. The blame for human ills is shifted to communal social sins and to the devil and his hierarchy of demons who are viewed as the instigators of every wrong act.

The terms frequently used are 'A New Vision', 'New Revelations' and 'Strategic Spiritual Warfare'. The practice used is the organization of prayer marches and 'Spiritual Mapping'. Trouble points are marked on a map (often with pins) and demons or demonic strongholds may be identified and targeted through spiritual warfare for attack. Gatekeepers are appointed to guard the entrances to cities, in order that the exorcised demons may not return. The city is claimed for Jesus, and the demons may not re-enter to mislead people.

Peter Wagner, born in 1930 and at one time professor of World Mission in Fuller Seminary, is the leader. He is the Head of Global Harvest Ministries whose office is in the World Prayer Center in Colorado Springs, Colorado, USA. He teaches that Satan sends senior demons from the hierarchy of evil spirits to control countries, regions, tribes, communities, residential areas and social networks in the world. Their main aim is to prevent the glorifying of God in their areas. They appoint demons of a lower rank to strengthen them in their attacks. This false teaching originates from the sect 'The Manifest Sons of God'.

During 1980, Wagner met John Wimber, founder of the Vineyard Movement. The Vineyard church became notorious for manifestations such as being slain in the spirit and laughing in the spirit, known also as the Toronto Blessing. Wagner was won over to the signs and wonders theology and its resulting charismatic revivals. He coined the term 'Third Wave'. Wagner says, 'The first wave was the Pentecostal movement, the second, the Charismatics, and now the Third Wave is joining them.' The 'Third Wave' is those conservative evangelicals now following after the signs and wonders movement.

Since then, Wagner moved steadily in the direction of the Manifested Sons of God theology as a result of his contact with 'prophets' like Paul Cain, Bill Hamon and Rick Joyner. He also made close contact with leaders from the Toronto/Brownsville Revival. Wagner wrote the preface for a book by Bill Hamon: *Apostles, Prophets and the Coming Moves of God: God's End-Time Plans for His Church and Planet Earth.*

We can be sure that Satan will be active to counterfeit the true with the false. This must not deter us from the pursuit of true revival.

The glorious possibility of revival

We should often reflect on the glorious possibility that we might soon come into a new age of revivals which will sweep from one nation to another. The sovereignty of God over the nations was evidenced in a remarkable way in the sudden revolution in Eastern Europe during November and December 1989. It was startling for its speed and power in instantly sweeping away over forty years of totalitarian atheistic Communism. It reminded us of the text: 'You will dash them to pieces like pottery' (Ps. 2:9). Let us think in terms of the omnipotence and glory of our triune God.

The Scripture promises assist us in this:

> From the west, men will fear the name of the Lord,
>   and from the rising of the sun, they will revere his glory
> For he will come like a pent-up flood
>   that the breath of the Lord drives along (Isa. 59:19).

> Who has ever heard such a thing?
>   Who has ever seen such things?
> Can a country be born in a day
>   or a nation be brought forth in a moment?
> Yet no sooner is Zion in labour
>   than she gives birth to her children (Isa 66:8).

How unique is that power of the Holy Spirit when he comes to glorify the son by giving to him the nations and the uttermost parts of the earth for his possession!

The citation of Joel 2:28-32 by the apostle Peter on the Day of Pentecost provides confirmation that we have the text before us as quoted by Peter:

> In the last days, God says,
>   I will pour out my Spirit on all people.
> Your sons and your daughters will prophesy,
>   your young men will see visions,
>   your old men will dream dreams.
> Even on my servants, both men and women,
>   I will pour out my Spirit in those days,
>   and they will prophesy.
> I will show wonders in the heaven above
>   and signs on the earth below,
>   blood and fire and billows of smoke.
> The sun will be turned to darkness
>   and the moon to blood
>   before the coming of the great and glorious day of the Lord.
> And everyone who calls
>   on the name of the Lord will be saved (Acts 2:17-21).

There are three specific predictions in the prophecy of Joel. The first is that there will be a radical upheaval in which the old order will be swept away. The second is that the new order will be one of revivals, with the Spirit being poured out on all flesh. This is the age of revivals in which 'Your sons and daughters will prophesy, your young men will see visions, your old men will dream dreams.' The third is that the way of salvation will be clear: 'And everyone who calls on the name of the Lord will be saved.' What could be clearer than salvation bestowed as a free gift — that is, justification by faith?

We should note well what is meant by the vivid imagery used, a form of speech we call apocalyptic language. The moon does not literally turn into blood nor do all our sons and daughters become prophets in the sense that Elijah or Moses were prophets. What it does mean is that there will be a glorious and universal clarity in knowing God, in understanding his Word, in the assurance of sins forgiven and in the joyful participation of the truth. 'They will all know me, from the least of them to the greatest', says the Lord (Heb. 8:11).

It is important to keep a clear view of the difference between the Old and New Covenant epochs. There is a unity and a discontinuity of the covenants, as we see in Hebrews 8 and 9. The Most Holy Place was entered once a year by the high priest. Now the way has been opened to the throne of grace so that all believers may approach our almighty God with confidence (Heb. 4:14-16). Yes, all true believers in the Old Testament were born again and justified by faith as we are (Rom. 4). There were spiritual revivals. The person and work of the Holy Spirit is clearly portrayed in chapters like Zechariah 4 and Ezekiel 37; yet there is in the gospel age a glorious clarity of truth and experience of salvation which far transcends the old order. The glory, joy and power of the gospel excited the crowds on that Day of Pentecost when 3,000 were added to the church. We should be excited by the fact that the power of the Holy Spirit is in no way diminished by the course of the centuries. Pentecost, although unique in some aspects, heralded in a new age. *This is the age of revivals*; this, our age, is the epoch of the pouring out of the Spirit on all peoples!

2. Give God no rest!

I have posted watchmen on your walls, O Jerusalem;
   they will never be silent day or night.
You who call on the LORD,
   give yourselves no rest,
   and give him no rest till he establishes Jerusalem
   and makes her the praise of the earth (Isa. 62:6-7).

In viewing the future glory of the church, Isaiah depicts her as being arrayed in robes of righteousness and spiritually prospering in such a way that all nations and kings will see her glory. Her righteousness will shine out like the dawn and her salvation will be like a blazing torch. She will be a crown of splendour in the Lord's hand (Isa. 62:1-5).

Today the church worldwide is weak and struggling, in spite of advancing into more places and nations than ever before. She faces defeat in many ways. Often she is inept, divided and feeble. Only heaven-sent revivals around the world can change the situation and give the church victory, making her 'the praise of the earth'.

God himself has instituted prayer as a means of grace. Although revival is usually preceded by prayer, we have in all humility to recognize that prayer too is a spiritual gift, something that cannot be created artificially or regimented. Therefore we are not to think that we can organize prayer as though we were in control. Certainly we should do all we can to make our regular prayer meetings informative, interesting and vital, at the same time seeking to stir up participation and zeal. Nevertheless, true

intercession cannot be measured in terms of good organization or
eloquence. The most powerful prayers have sometimes consisted
of the groans of God's suffering, persecuted people. Desperate
cries made out of weakness have proved to be the most effec-
tual prayers (Ps. 102:17; Exod. 3:7; Dan. 9:17-19; Neh. 9:32-
37). Our present weakness and discouragements may be turned
to our advantage as we pray, remembering that it is the Lord's
name that is at stake and his cause that is contested by the powers of evil. In our feebleness we must recall that he is strong and
full of sympathy:

> The Lord will judge his people
>   and have compassion on his servants
> when he sees their strength is gone
>   and no-one is left, slave or free (Deut 32:36).

and again,

> I looked, but there was no-one to help,
>   I was appalled that no-one gave support;
> so my own arm worked salvation for me (Isa. 63:5).

The very ability to pray with unction and faith is given by the
Holy Spirit, and although that activity largely precedes revival, it is
also part of it: 'And I will pour out on the house of David and the
inhabitants of Jerusalem a spirit of grace and supplication. They
will look on me, the one they have pierced, and they will mourn
for him as one mourns for an only child' (Zech. 12:10).

If we return to Isaiah 62:6-7, which was quoted at the beginning of this chapter, we can observe three salient points.

1. The watchmen are posted by the Lord

It is the Lord himself who posts the watchmen on the walls of Jerusalem. The duties of a watchman are described in the commission given to Ezekiel, who was made a watchman for the house
of Israel (Ezek. 33). Ezekiel was not only to warn all to turn from
their wicked ways and so avoid death, but he was also to interpret

providence to them, such as the fall of Jerusalem. In other words, he was to be their eyes and ears, spiritually speaking. A watchman is just that. He blows the trumpet of warning at the first sign of enemy approach. He also watches for messengers of peace. His task is not only negative, but positive as well. The watchmen are to know the times and needs of God's people. They are to inspire and direct them and to call them to repentance and prayer. They are to heed and interpret the promises, and then plead fervently for their fulfilment.

2. They believe that Jerusalem will be made the praise of the earth

These watchmen posted on the walls by the Lord believe that, in spite of all the weakness and smallness of the cause they represent, the glory of the Messiah is bound up in it. They know that it is the absolute determination of the Lord whom they serve to promote the glory of his Son. In spite of all his enemies, he will make his cause, which is also their cause, the praise of the earth. These watchmen are interpreters of God's promises. They see that, following the death and resurrection of the Messiah, he is exalted to the highest place, from where he will exercise his power on earth until his enemies are made his footstool (Ps. 110:1). Then he will appear in his great Second Coming and utterly destroy our worst enemy, which is death (1 Cor. 15:25-26).

Having bound Satan, that strong man, this mighty Lord of life despoils his kingdom, so locking him up that he is no longer able to deceive the nations (Rev. 20:1-3). Expositors such as William Hendriksen, David Chilton and Grant R. Osborne see Revelation 20:1-6 as the whole period from Christ's first coming to his second coming and 1,000 years as a symbolic expression of the fulness of that time. During that whole period all God's people, united to him by faith, reign with Christ. His cause is theirs; his victory is theirs too. When his cause is shamed, they too are shamed. The Son of God did not immediately bring about the undeceiving of the nations. That is a progressive work, for he will go on reigning and exercising dominion until his enemies become his footstool. Some nations, especially Islamic nations like Saudi Arabia, are impenetrable as far as the gospel is concerned. All gospel activity is forbidden. But the watchmen must give the Lord no rest until these nations are liberated and made free for the gospel.

3. They give the Lord no rest

These watchmen are so confident that Jerusalem will be made the praise of the earth that they give themselves no rest in prayer, and they give the Lord no rest, until he comes and makes it so. Note that these watchmen are motivated by the promises of God. It is precisely because they believe that the Lord has promised that Jerusalem will be made the praise of the earth that they give themselves no rest about the matter. We are not to think of these watchmen as being obsessed with one idea only. Ezekiel was a watchman; so was Daniel. They were both exceedingly hardworking: Ezekiel was a busy pastor, and Daniel was a high-ranking statesman. Few in this world are more pressed than men of that calibre. Yet we can see from the Scriptures that they always bore in their hearts the state of God's cause. That was uppermost in their minds and prominent in their prayers. Our daily prayers encompass many burdens as we seek faithfully to remember churches, situations and individuals. This inevitably requires discipline and order if we are to have meaningful prayer lives. Yet such is our desire for the glory of our triune God that we are incessant, or should be incessant, in our prayers for revival. Is that so? The very Word of Yahweh requires it. He says, 'Give yourselves no rest until I make Jerusalem the praise of the earth' (from Isa. 62:7). That is, take my promises seriously! Do not give up!

We are to remember what our Lord said about the persistent widow. Her cause was a just one; she had a right to ask. She knew that and she kept asking without giving up. In present-day terms imagine a man being telephoned every day about a problem; whether at office or at home, there is no escape. This is just too much! Even though he is a worldly man, one who does not fear God and does not really care about the outcome, he will grant what is requested to get rid of the nuisance.

When we pray, we come to one who does care and who is just. Our cause is righteous and concerns our great, omnipotent God, who loves us and cares for us in a most fatherly way. We often miss the point of what Jesus says in this illustration: 'Will he keep putting them off? I tell you, he will see that they get justice, and quickly' (Luke 18:7-8). But, sadly, the fact is that few are like that woman who kept up with her request. Our Lord asks the question: 'When the Son of Man comes, will he find faith on the earth?' (Luke 18:8). The question surely, in the context, is: will he find that kind of persevering, believing faith, like that of the widow woman? The coming referred to does not need to be the great final Second Coming because the Lord also comes to the earth in judgements and revivals. The verb used is a common one for coming (elthon) and is not necessarily associated with the great unveiling, or the final appearing of Christ. Peter speaks of persevering through suffering, so that when the Lord visits us on the day of revival there will be those who, coming to faith, will give him glory for the testimony of faithful believers (1 Peter 2:12).

Whenever he comes, even if it is today, will he find that faith, the faith which perseveres, the faith of this widow? (See Hendriksen's commentary on Luke.) If we do apply the text to the final Second Coming of our Lord, it would certainly not mean that there will be no Christians on the earth, but rather that cold winds might be blowing, as they were when the letter to the Hebrews was written to warn against apostasy. Will there then be that living tenacious faith that believes absolutely and keeps on unfalteringly without giving up?

Not giving ourselves rest implies that we are to take the promises of God very seriously. We are never to give up on them. Moreover we must not tire or relent in our prayers. As watchmen we must be very well informed about the needs of God's cause and exceedingly persistent in our intercessions.

But will this not be tedious? Surely we must not be repetitious? Won't the Lord become bored with our incessant petitioning? His answer is clear. He says, 'You who call on the LORD ... give him no rest till he establishes Jerusalem and makes her the praise of the earth' (Isa. 62:6-7). Only when he has accomplished that, need you think about giving up. We are to be scrupulous about the meaning of his Word. He says 'the praise of the earth', not 'a praise of the earth'. We are not to be content with a remnant mentality.

It simply is not good enough that true Christianity is relegated to the league of cults and sects, or that in some nations, for example, Italy, Jehovah's Witnesses outnumber evangelicals. Only powerful heaven-sent revivals of the kind that have already adorned the history of the church can possibly redress the situation worldwide today.

3. Jonathan Edwards (1703-1758)
— theologian of revival

In his famous book *The Mystery of Providence,* the Puritan John Flavel stresses the importance of noting outstanding events in our lives. He declares, 'The remembrance of former providences will minister to our souls continual matter of praise and thanksgiving, which is the very employment of the angels in heaven, and the sweetest part of our lives on earth.'[1]

Of exceptional encouragement to Edwards was the entrance into his life of David Brainerd — a matter on which he often reflected. It was on Thursday, 28 May 1747, at the time when Edwards was preparing for publication of the treatise calling for a concert of prayer, that David Brainerd rode into the parsonage yard at Northampton. Edwards, whose mind was engaged in the vision of worldwide mission, had only met Brainerd once before. Now, through close contact, he was to share much more deeply in the experience of labouring among the Indians, particularly with a detailed knowledge of the spiritual awakening among them. The story of Brainerd is a profoundly moving one: his struggle with the disease which was to claim his life, his wrestling with the total depravity and rejection of the gospel by the Indians, his near despair on that account, and above all his transparent godliness.

Although limited in physical strength, Brainerd gave himself unremittingly and sacrificially to the Indians among whom he was eventually to witness a phenomenal spiritual awakening. He died of tuberculosis in Edwards' home at the early age of twenty-nine, leaving his journals in Edwards' possession. These diaries formed the basis of Edwards' biography of Brainerd, which in due course became by far his most popular book. It is reckoned that this was the first missionary biography to be printed in America. Some believe it has made a greater impact on the church for the cause of missions than any other. It was the revival among the Indians that gave power to this biography and is gripping in interest.

Of course there were many other aspects of providence which equipped Edwards to write on revival. He witnessed revival in his church at Northampton in 1735, and again a few years later when revival spread more widely across New England during the years 1740 to 1742, during which time he came to know George Whitefield.

These events in and of themselves would not adequately explain the role of Edwards as 'the theologian of revival'. He was endowed with a brilliant intellect which included an aptitude for analysis. His early development was evident inasmuch as he was proficient in Latin at the age of six. He possessed an astute theological and philosophical mind. Concentration was a discipline in which he excelled. When not away in travel he would spend thirteen hours a day in the study. Francis Bacon said, 'Reading maketh a full man, conference a ready man, and writing an exact man.'[2] The latter was certainly true of Edwards. Writing was his forte. He made it a rule to think clearly first and then write precisely. When eventually his papers were collected, it was found to be difficult to grade his materials into first and second degree categories. They were all of the same uniform high quality. Naturally some of the themes upon which he wrote are of more relevance to us now than others.

Edwards was a Puritan in theology and practice. He not only fully concurred with the Puritans in their Reformed theology of salvation, but also shared their emphasis on the centrality of practical and experimental Christianity.

Edwards' brilliant mind and remarkable exegetical acumen equipped him for the task of describing and defending revivals. Historians have accorded to him the reputation of being the finest theologian in American history. His textual work and sermons show that he was a proficient expositor of Scripture. For instance, he preached a series of sermons on justification, in which he expertly defended that truth from the error of introducing human merit on account of faith.

In all Edwards wrote five treatises on revival. The first was *A Narrative of Surprising Conversions,* which describes the revival in Northampton in 1735 in which 300 souls were added to the church. The second was *Thoughts on the Revival in New England in 1740,* the third *The Distinguishing Marks of a Work of the Spirit of God* (1741), the fourth *A History of the Work of Redemption* (1744) and the fifth, which was his deepest and fullest work, *The Religious Affections* (1746). The last-named was really a development of the third title listed above. To these treatises we should add the biography of Brainerd, because of the revival among the Indians described in it, which in a very graphic way highlights the sovereign grace of God. Humanly speaking there seemed no hope whatsoever of the grace of God breaking through the darkness and enmity which held the Indians in Satan's vice.

J. I. Packer, in a paper given at the Puritan Conference in London in 1961, helpfully summed up Edwards' teaching on revival under three headings which, with a few principal comments of explanation we set out in the following paragraphs:[3]

1. Revival is an extraordinary work of God the Holy Ghost reinvigorating and propagating Christian piety in a community.

Revival is an extraordinary work, because it marks the abrupt reversal of an established trend and state of things among those who profess to be God's people. To envisage God reviving his church is to presuppose that the church has previously grown moribund and gone to sleep.

2. Revivals have a central place in the revealed purposes of God.

'The end of God's creating the world', declares Edwards, 'was to prepare a kingdom for his Son (for he was appointed heir of the world).' This end is to be realized, first through Christ's accomplished redemption on Calvary, and then through the triumphs of his kingdom. 'All the dispensations of God's providence henceforward (since Christ's ascension), even to the final consummation of all things, are to give Christ his reward, and fulfil his end in what he did and suffered upon earth.' A universal dominion is pledged to Christ and in the interim, before the final consummation, the Father implements this pledge in part by successive outpourings of the Spirit, which prove the reality of Christ's kingdom to a sceptical world and serve to extend its bounds among Christ's erstwhile enemies.

3. Revivals are the most glorious of all God's works in the world.

Edwards insists on this, to shame those who professed no interest in the divine awakening that had come to New England, and insinuated by their attitude that a Christian's mind could be more profitably occupied with other matters.

'Such a work is, in its nature and kind, the most glorious of any work of God whatsoever', Edwards protests. 'It is the work of redemption (the great end of all the other works of God, and of which the work of creation was but a shadow). It is the work of new creation, which is infinitely more glorious than the old. I am bold to say that the work of God in the conversion of one soul ... is a more glorious work than the creation of the whole material universe.'[4]

Having outlined the subject in general, Edwards deals with three particular subjects related to revival which are particularly relevant for us today.

1. Satan's tactics in revivals

The first and worst enemy in revivals is spiritual pride. The adversary is the Prince of pride. 'This is the main door by which the devil comes into the hearts of those who are zealous for the advancement of religion. It is the chief inlet of smoke from the bottomless pit.' Giving to human instruments the glory due to God alone is a curse to be avoided. Edwards urges the necessity of humility and cites Psalm 25:9: 'The meek will he guide in judgement and the meek he will teach his way.' He points out too that the spiritually proud man is beyond correction because he esteems himself to be full of spiritual light already.[5]

The next warning, in which Edwards addresses the question of prophecies and visions which claim to have been given by direct inspiration, could hardly be more apposite for us today. By such a notion the devil has a great door opened for him, because once this principle of inspiration is accepted, Satan has the opportunity to have his word regarded as the infallible rule, and can soon bring the Bible into neglect and contempt.

With heightened levels of spiritual experience in revival, the temptation comes to make more of passionate inward experiences than is warranted. Satan will especially tempt some to think they are converted because they are convicted of sin, but conviction is not the same as repentance. Edwards points out that inward experience is a mixed thing. It is not necessarily pure and without self-interest.

Even the most exalted spiritual experiences can have defects. With hindsight, passionate experiences can often be recognized as having carnal elements. That the ultimate proof of genuine experience is the fruit of the Spirit and sound Christian practice is firmly established in his treatise *The Religious Affections,* where the theme of experience is extensively analysed.

2. The apostolic gifts and miracles have ceased

This issue has been debated in great detail during the 1980s. Some have claimed with great confidence that it is impossible to establish from Scripture that tongues and prophecies have ceased. The idea has prevailed that no self-respecting expositor would dare to uphold the cessation of tongues and prophecies on the basis of 1 Corinthians 13. In his book *Charity and Its Fruits,* Edwards did not attempt to do that exegetically in the way that Douglas Judisch does in his *An Evaluation of Claims to the Charismatic Gifts* or Victor Budgen does in his book *Charismatics and the Word of God.* Edwards is believed to have written a detailed exegesis of 1 Corinthians 13 in an unpublished work, but in *Charity and Its Fruits* he simply asserts the orthodox position concerning the cessation of tongues, miracles and prophecies, and then expounds on the fact that grace and love are infinitely more excellent than special gifts designed to accompany the establishment of the Scriptures. That, to Edwards, is the message of 1 Corinthians 13. That is what Paul was seeking to impress on the minds of the believers at Corinth.[6]

It is a fact that there is a constant tendency to be preoccupied with phenomena. A weak faith desires proofs of God. A strong faith rests in the authority of Scripture and the perfect and completed work of Christ. In revival there is the ever-present danger of concentrating on the spectacular and the outward, being excited about crowds or sensational features such as the conversion of a famous person, or, as has been the case in parts of Indonesia, being largely taken up with healings. At the end of the day, however, it is progressive sanctification that counts. The more Christians are obsessed with the outward and external, the less they will concentrate on the Word which alone is able to build them up and make them strong in Christ.

3. Prayer for revival

Besides his *Humble Attempt* treatise seeking to promote the concert of prayer for revival, Edwards stresses the importance of intercession in *Thoughts on Revival*. He reasons there that the great and glorious work that had been witnessed was in itself a major reason to pray for yet greater things. He goes on to maintain 'that it is God's will that the prayers of his people should be one great principal means of carrying on the designs of Christ's kingdom in the world'. He continues:

> When God has something very great to accomplish for his church, it is his will that there should precede it the extraordinary prayers of his people; as is manifest by Ezekiel 36:37: 'I will yet for this be inquired of by the house of Israel, to do this for them.' And it is revealed that, when God is about to accomplish great things for his church, he will begin by a remarkable pouring out of the spirit of grace and supplication (Zech. 12:10). If we are not to expect that the devil should go out of a particular person, under a bodily possession, without extraordinary prayer, or prayer and fasting; how much less should we expect to have him cast out of the land, and the world, without it![7]

How, then, should we pray for worldwide revival? As we have just seen, if the devil is to be cast out of his strongholds there will be need for prayer and fasting by the church.

Edwards had an extensive vision for the world of the mid-eighteenth century. The world of that time was much smaller that our twenty-first century world. If Edwards could have read what is now a bedside book for many, namely *Operation World*, he would have been amazed. Today we can have at our command detailed knowledge of every nation and province under the sun, forty to fifty times more than could have been assembled in the year 1750. How does this affect the way in which we pray?

Part of the answer is that we should respond to the needs that surround us. It is helpful for carefully prepared information, nation by nation, to precede times of prayer. We should think in terms of much more time being devoted to such exercises and for churches to come together for special seasons of prayer. An example has already been afforded in this by those who have organized weeks of prayer, in which times have been designated to pray for up to thirty different nations. It is important to appreciate that while the principles involved in revival are always the same, nevertheless God moves in unexpected ways. He works in various ways in different societies and every revival has stamped on it 'Made in Heaven'. This feature of divine originality is important. In timing and in style, every revival has divine genius as its hallmark. When we look at revivals in history we are constrained to stand back and say, 'This could not have been done by men, nor could men at their best ever have conceived of such spiritual creations — which is what true revivals are in essence.'

We should prepare for times when the heavens will be opened and the promises realize their fulfilment. Surely it is our responsibility not only to pray for revivals, but to prepare ourselves theologically for them. Here it is that Edwards' writings are so useful to us. As he held the glory of God to be the supreme end of all things, so ought we. 'For from him and through him and to him are all things. To him be the glory for ever, Amen' (Rom. 11:36).

4. Broadening definitions of revivals

Two thousand five hundred gathered in Minneapolis in October 2003 to celebrate the 300th anniversary of the birth of Jonathan Edwards (1703-1758) who is esteemed by many as the greatest philosopher-theologian of American history. Eleven audio cassette recordings emanated from that memorable conference. A book writing up the materials of the conference was published in 2004 with the title *A God Entranced Vision of All Things: The Legacy of Jonathan Edwards.* J. I. Packer's contribution in this book is to explore the mind of Edwards on the subject of revival. In doing so Packer shows that Edwards' theology of revival is perhaps the most important single contribution that Edwards has made to evangelical thinking today. So far we have considered definitions of revivals. Just what revival is can be broadened in scope and this is how Packer expresses that broadening:

> What exactly happens in a reviving visitation from God, gradual or sudden, brief or prolonged, large or small scale, as the case may be? From the archetypal revival era, we can put together a general answer to that question, all the specifics of which can be illustrated, one way or another, from Edwards' revival writings. To be sure, no two episodes of revival are identical, if only because the various individuals and communities to which, and the various cultural backgrounds against which, the reviving of religion takes place have their own unique features, and in every narrative of revival these should be noted. But the same generic pattern appears everywhere. Revival is God touching minds and hearts in an arresting, devastating, exalting way, to draw them to himself, through working from the inside out rather than from the outside in. It is God accelerating, intensifying, and extending the work of grace that goes on in every Christian's life, but is sometimes overshadowed and somewhat smothered by the impact of other forces. It is the near presence of God giving new power to the gospel. It is the Holy Spirit sensitizing souls to divine realities and so generating deep-level re-

sponses to God in the form of faith and repentance, praise and prayer, love and joy, works of benevolence, and service, and initiatives of outreach and sharing.[8]

Packer goes on to outline the ingredients that are intensified in revival, which are here summarized:[9]

1. God's holy presence is sensed and felt as our hearts are searched.
2. God's Word penetrates with power.
3. Conviction of sin is deeply felt.
4. Repentance runs deep (Zech 12:10ff; John 16:8-11).
5. Christ's cross is valued.
6. Reformation in life and behaviour is advanced.
7. Love breaks out, 'The town seemed to be full of the presence of God: it never was so full of love as then'.
8. Joy fills hearts.
9. Churches are revived.
10. Satan makes his counter-attacks.

These definitions stir us to pray for revivals in every nation of the world. We must pray for revivals in seminaries, colleges, schools, denominations, and among groups of people as they are evangelized for the first time (such as when David Brainerd evangelized the Indians). Nothing less than this can sufficiently glorify our Lord Jesus Christ.

The Glory of God in Revival

The glory of the triune God is displayed in revival. Christ is glorified because 'He shall see of the travail of his soul, and shall be satisfied' (Isa. 53:11, KJV). The reward for his work will be seen on a global scale (Ps. 22:27-31). He must be honoured by all nations and tribes, and people of every language (Ps. 2:8, 9; Ps. 67; Isa. 49:6, 7; Rev 7:9).

The glory of God is heightened in individuals during revival. Jonathan Edwards described his experience of the glory of God when he was in his late teens:

The first instance that I remember of that sort of inward, sweet delight in God and divine things, that I have lived much in since, was on reading those words, 1 Tim. 1:17, 'Now unto the King, eternal, immortal, invisible, the only wise God, be honour and glory forever and ever, Amen.' As I read these words, there came into my soul, and was as it were diffused through it a sense of the glory of the Divine Being; a new sense, quite different from anything I ever experienced before.[10]

Writing on the theme of glory, John Piper testifies as follows:

No one in Church history with the possible exception of St Augustine has shown more clearly and shockingly (starkly) the infinite importance of joy in the very essence of what it means for God to be God and what it means for us to be God glorifying. Joy always seemed to me peripheral until I read Edwards. He simply transformed my universe by putting joy at the centre of what it means for God to be God and what it means for us to be God-glorifying.[11]

There is a description of the effects of revival which illustrates beautifully the blessings that follow and the outpouring of the Holy Spirit. This is found in a small book by Handley Moule where he writes of his early life and experiences in the parish of Fordington, near Dorchester, where his father was the Vicar from 1829 until his decease in 1880, some fifty years later. He writes:

I must not close without a memory, however meagre, of one wonderful epoch in the parish. It was the Revival. The year was 1859, 'that year of the right hand of the Most High', when, beginning with a noon prayer meeting in the premises of a church in New York, a spiritual movement wide and marvellous spread over the States, was felt in the West Indies, and touched even ships on the Atlantic, so that once and again a liner reached New York 'with a revival on board' which had originated on the voyage. Ulster was profoundly and lastingly moved and blessed. Here and there in England it was the same; and Fordington was one of the scenes of the divine awakening. For surely it was divine. No artificial means of excitement were dreamt of; my Father's whole genius was against it. No powerful personality, no Moody or Aitken, came to us. A city-missionary and a London Bible-woman were the only helpers from a distance. But a power not of man brought souls to ask the old question, 'What must I do to be saved?' Up and down the village the pastor and the pastoress, and their faithful helpers, as they went their daily rounds, found the 'anxious'. And the Church was thronged to overflowing, and so was the spacious schoolroom, night after night throughout the week. The very simplest means carried with them a heavenly power. The plain reading of a chapter often conveyed the call of God to men and women, and they 'came to Jesus as they were'.

I do not think I exaggerate when I say that hundreds of people at that time were awakened, awed, made conscious of eternal realities. And a goodly number of these showed in all their after life that they were indeed new creatures, born again to a living hope and to a steadfast walk. And 'the leaves of the trees were for healing', apart from its holy fruit of spiritual conversions. A great social uplifting, wholesome and permanent, followed the Revival. In particular, a vigorous movement for temperance and thrift arose spontaneously among the work people, and was wisely fostered and organised by my Father and his friends.[12]

This revival which swept America brought an amazing change in England in which the church membership of the Church of England increased from 18 percent of the population to 27 percent.

4. The centrality of gospel preaching in revival

There are many who believe that revival will come through the restoration of miraculous signs and wonders to the churches. Some believe that this restoration includes the recovery of the apostolic office. However, that is not the main point. The crucial issue is the belief that all nine supernatural gifts described in 1 Corinthians 12:7-11 should continue and that the church should pray for miraculous signs and wonders to be done (Acts 4:30).

Those who disagree with that position follow the theology of the English Puritans like John Owen and in particular Jonathan Edwards. They believe in the triumph of the gospel worldwide through gospel preaching accompanied by outpourings of the Holy Spirit in revival. The important difference is that they believe this will take place without the restoration of the nine extraordinary gifts outlined in 1 Corinthians 12:7-11. They believe that the power lies in the preaching of Christ and the application of the gospel without any addition of supernatural healings and miracles. It is not that they do not believe that God can perform extraordinary healings and miracles today. Revivals can bring in their wake extraordinary miracles, but such things are absolutely secondary to the great central issue of the gospel. It is the gospel which is the power of God to salvation, not miracles or signs (Rom. 1:16-17). The children of Israel witnessed extraordinary miracles such as the dividing of the Red Sea in their deliverance from Egypt and the giving of the law at Mount Sinai, but seeing miracles does not regenerate human hearts. The worship of the golden calf showed that the minds and hearts of the Israelites was mostly unaffected by the miracles. It is by the truth of law and gospel that the Holy Spirit brings regeneration.

Throughout the history of the church there have been those who have claimed to be able to perform miracles, but these have not stood up to real testing. In his book, *Miracles Yesterday and Today*,[1] B. B. Warfield examines this question in a thoroughly investigative and documentative manner. Those who dislike Warfield's position speak in a derogatory way about this book yet hardly answer his thesis. Warfield's work is worthy of study. In a thoroughly scholarly manner he examines the patristic period, Roman Catholic claims, Edward Irving and so-called faith healing.

With the present-day situation in mind it is necessary to look afresh at the book of Acts, for it is there that we have the narratives which describe the first revivals. An examination of Acts will also reveal the prime place given to preaching Christ. He is the centre. But it is impossible to preach Christ without expounding the nature of God and of the Trinity in particular. We are required by the Great Commission to baptize converts in the name of the three persons, which presupposes that they have an adequate understanding of the Trinity. This raises the question: what are the principal truths which are central to every revival?

As we shall see, it is only a recovery of the gospel itself, together with spiritual awakenings, that is sufficient to conquer the forces of the world, sin and darkness, and Satan. It is the gospel which should occupy our devoted attention, and not efforts to speak in tongues or strivings to enter a new age of prophecy and miracles. In Christ the prophecies are fulfilled and in him Scripture is sealed and complete, as predicted by Daniel. Moreover the resurrection of Christ is our miracle, ten thousand times more relevant and important than preoccupation with healing our aches and pains.

1. The book of Acts

The book of Acts occupies a unique position in the New Testament. It is the only account of the establishment and growth of the apostolic church. It provides the key to understanding the background of Paul's letters and is the link between the four Gospels and the rest of the New Testament. It would seem that most commentaries concentrate on the exegesis of the text and miss the main thrust of the message of Acts. Why is so little attention given to exposition of the progress of the church and missions? Often it is disappointing to find an inadequate development and discussion of the great issues,[2] such as the power involved in spiritual awakening.

For instance, this is the thrust of Acts 1:8: 'But you will receive power when the Holy Spirit comes upon you.' Uppermost in the minds of the disciples was political power. But these apostles were to be anointed with the Holy Spirit and clothed with heavenly power to enable them to witness about what they had seen and heard. They would be empowered to be effective preachers. The same Holy Spirit that had come upon Jesus to anoint him for his ministry would be with them, filling their minds and hearts, and at the same time working powerfully in those who would hear their preaching. This is the power we associate with revival.

Up to the twenty-first chapter, Acts is a record of revivals, beginning with Pentecost. Several factors related to revival call for comment.

First, there is the factor of *preparation*. The ministry of our Lord provided the preparation for those revivals. My principal concern in this book is to draw attention to our need to pray for, and prepare for, a spiritual awakening. Revivals are preceded by prayer, study and outreach. The 120 were well prepared for the work which was suddenly thrust upon them.

Secondly, there is the factor of *spiritual power*. The Holy Spirit came as a baptism (a baptism by its very nature occurs once only) upon the 120 at Pentecost and later upon non-Jewish groups: the Samaritans (Acts 8), the Gentiles of Cornelius' household (Acts 10), and the pagan Gentiles far off at Ephesus (Acts 19). There was a special unction in the preaching, both in the inspiration of the contents of what was said and in the direct way it was applied to the hearers. Many times of filling or empowerment of the Spirit followed Pentecost (Acts 4:31). The coming of the Spirit in might to empower the preachers and to regenerate sinners is characteristic of revival.

Thirdly, there is the factor of *opposition*. All the way through Acts we observe the conflict between the believing church and the unbelieving Jews and their leaders. The same Sanhedrin (the main tribunal or council of seventy elders representing the supreme religious authority in Jerusalem) which condemned Jesus also persecuted the apostles and had them flogged (Acts 5:40). That same Sanhedrin heard Stephen's defence and then went wild in their fury and stoned him to death. We see too in the missionary journeys of Paul (Acts 12:25; 21:17) the way in which Satan stirred up pagan opposition, creating riots and confusion in an attempt to impede the progress of the gospel.

Fourthly, there were the *consequences* of revival. All kinds of controversies resulted from the revivals. Where life is created the problems of growth and nurture follow. For instance, Corinth was a large city notorious for its corruption and vice. There a substantial church came into being through the preaching of the gospel. Paul's letters to the Corinthians reveal a wide variety of daunting doctrinal and practical problems. Most pastors today, if faced with such a set of difficulties, would conclude that the position was hopeless, but Paul, with the tenacity typical of him, faced every one of them squarely. It is evident that in spite of the problems which beset the newly planted churches, missionary outreach and enterprises were born. For instance, from the church in Ephesus churches were planted all over Asia Minor. Such missionary enterprise is typical of revival.

Fifthly, there is the *transitory nature* of Acts. The Gospels and Acts describe the period of transition between the Old Testament and the New. This is a matter of very great significance. The mighty signs, wonders and miracles of Jesus and his apostles belonged peculiarly to that period and were specifically designed to attest the reality of Jesus as Son of God, and especially point to and confirm the reality of his resurrection from the dead and exaltation to God's right hand.

These features, together with the apostolic office, the ceremonial laws, Levitical sacrifices and theocratic laws, all passed away. It is the saving gospel alone that continues — the gospel which is God's power to salvation to everyone who believes, and will be to the end of time (Rom. 1:16-17; Matt. 28:18-20).

Sixthly, there is the *character of the preaching*, to which we now turn.

2. Preaching Christ in a revival

It is thrilling to observe the clarity and conviction with which the apostles testified to the glory of Christ both in his person and work. The book of Hebrews is preeminent in extolling the supremacy of Jesus as Prophet, Priest, King and Administrator of a new and better covenant. Christ is central in Peter's sermon at Pentecost.

First, Peter testified to the *nature of Jesus as Son of God*. The Father exalted him to his right hand and the outcome and proof of that was the outpouring of the Holy Spirit, as all present could see for themselves.

Secondly, Peter testified to the *perfect life and ministry of Christ*. There could be no doubt about his identity as the Messiah: 'Men of Israel, listen to this: Jesus of Nazareth was a man accredited by God to you by miracles, wonders and signs, which God did among you through him' (Acts 2:22).

Thirdly, Peter testified to his *extraordinary death*, which was predestined by God, but which was engineered and instigated by the Jewish leaders who rejoiced in his betrayal, rejection and humiliation. They were responsible for his being handed over to the agony of crucifixion, which was executed by violent men.

Fourthly, Peter testified that God had reversed the rejection of his Son, demonstrating this by his glorious resurrection from the dead. This resurrection was predicted in Psalm 16. It was impossible for God's Holy One to see decay. Yes, God raised him from the dead, and Peter drove home the point with the words of testimony: 'And we are all witnesses of the fact' (Acts 2:32).

Fifthly, Peter testified to the *exaltation of Jesus*. This is expressed in some detail. Jesus is exalted to the right hand of God. They had sought to sink him to the lowest pit of degradation and would gladly have looked down on his mutilated corpse in the valley of Gehenna, but to their consternation they had to look upwards to see him seated in victory in the highest conceivable place of honour and glory. Such is his power that the superlative gift of the person of the Holy Spirit comes only by his will and request.

Sixthly, Peter testified to the *immediate saving power of Jesus*. Each point logically leads to the next. Since our Lord now occupies the supreme place of authority he is in a position to apply his own work as Redeemer. Peter can assure forgiveness to all those who repent and show their repentance in baptism. This assurance or promise is strengthened by the quotation from Joel: 'Everyone who calls on the name of the Lord will be saved.'

Seventhly, Peter testified to *the discipleship of Jesus*. Peter called on all those who repented to identify with the new community, the church of which Christ alone is the head. Discipleship means adherence and obedience to a leader. The new believers would not be left in isolation, but would be joined together in a caring body whose Chief Shepherd was Jesus.

It is acknowledged by all commentators that the book of Acts includes many sermons or speeches which together add up to about a quarter of the contents. Every one of these is evangelistic in approach except the address of Paul to the Ephesian elders reported in Acts 20. What is recorded for us in Acts contains the salient points, as Luke says of this first sermon, 'With many other words he warned them; and he pleaded with them.' In other words, we are given the outline. We can be sure that no truth was withheld when the apostles were plied with questions.

3. The principal truths preached in revivals

We have seen that Peter preached Christ comprehensively as the one who has fulfilled all the promises of redemption and who is reigning now as King to give salvation to both Jews and Gentiles. The Old Testament is the book of promise about Christ, and the New Testament is the exposition of Christ as living Redeemer. It is the business of the gospel preacher to preach Christ from all the Scriptures. It matters little what part of the Bible is used. For instance, in a famous revival in 1630 at a place called Shotts in Scotland, John Livingstone preached Christ from Ezekiel 36:25: 'And I will sprinkle clean water upon you and you will be clean.' Later about 500 souls attributed their spiritual awakening to that sermon.

While it is required of gospel preachers that they preach the whole counsel of God and hide nothing which he has revealed in his holy and infallible Word, there are some truths which particularly stand out, especially in times of revival, when the Holy Spirit is working in unusual power. I will refer to several of these under the following headings.

The holiness of God

The reality of hell is included under this heading. The holy character of God is declared by his love of righteousness and his hatred of wickedness (Heb. 1:9). The Day of Pentecost was charged with the presence of the living, holy God coming in majestic power to vindicate the cause of his Son. Frivolity is inconceivable in the presence of a holy God whose wrath rests upon impenitent sinners. In revival the reality of eternal punishment is not only preached; it is felt in an awesome manner. Peter pleaded with sinners to flee for their lives from the wrath to come. In times of religious declension, gospel clowns flourish and entertainment is welcomed. But in times of spiritual awakening there is a renewed sense of the holiness of God.

Justification by faith alone

Faith is the instrument by which sinners are brought to Christ and joined to him. In this union their sin is removed once and for all and Christ's righteousness put to their account. The one united to Christ is constituted legally righteous by the imputation of Christ's righteousness. Faith is not the meritorious ground of acceptance. Peter did not imply that those who believed would be showing their own goodness in doing so, but rather that by believing they could be joined to one who alone is good. It is important to note the fulness and perfection of Christ's righteousness. In him is no sin. Not only so, but by his life and obedience, he has fulfilled all righteousness. He is the believing sinner's righteousness (Jer. 23:6). The importance of this can hardly be exaggerated. Nothing less than perfect righteousness can satisfy the Father, who is glorious in holiness, and nothing less can satisfy the sinner's conscience when it is overwhelmed with a sense of guilt and appalled by a sense of helplessness. When sin condemns and Satan accuses, what is my plea but that Jesus died for me? Is that not enough? Is the blood of Jesus not enough to cleanse away my sin? Is the perfect righteousness of

Christ not enough to constitute the sinner righteous before God? What? The life and death of Jesus combined, not enough? Our Father says that his Son's propitiation is enough! (Rom. 3:25; 1 John 2:2; 4:10). Then who can condemn me if the Father of our Lord Jesus Christ justifies me? (Rom. 8:33).

In revivals deep conviction of sin is felt. Indeed some are terrified by the holiness of God and by the condemning power of the moral law, for by the law is a knowledge of sin (Rom. 3:19-20). Yet it is vital to stress that it is not terrors, or convictions, or qualifications of any kind in the sinner that give him a right to receive mercy. The First London Confession of Faith, drawn up by seven Baptist churches in 1644 and republished in 1646, addressed this question: 'The preaching of the gospel to the conversion of sinners, is absolutely free; no way requiring as absolutely necessary, any qualification, preparations, or terrors of the law, or preceding ministry of the law but only and alone the naked 'soul, a sinner and ungodly, to receive Christ crucified, dead and buried, and risen again; who is made a prince and a Saviour for such sinners as through the gospel shall be brought to believe in him' (article 25). The proof texts provided are John 3:14-15; 1:12; Isa. 55:1; John 7:37; 1 Tim. 1:15; Rom. 4:5; 5:8; Acts 5:30-31; 2:36; 1 Cor. 1:22,24.

The reason why this is vital in revival is because when conviction of sin is intense the questions arise: 'Have I sorrowed enough? Have I repented enough? Have I qualified to receive forgiveness?' But salvation, as stated above, is absolutely free of conditions. My only warrant to believe on Christ and receive him is the command of God to do so. The Philippian jailer in Acts 16 was desperate. He was evidently spiritually awakened. He cried out, 'Sirs, what must I do to be saved?' They replied, 'Believe in the Lord Jesus, and you will be saved,—,you and your household' (Acts 16:31). Why did they not include repentance when it is mentioned as essential in so many other places? The answer is surely self-evident: namely, that he was already showing repentance. However, repentance is a great issue in revival and we must examine that too.

The call to repentance

The Old Testament prophets preached repentance. John the Baptist preached repentance (Mark 1:4). Jesus began his ministry with the call to repentance (Mark 1:15). 'Unless you repent,' he declared, 'you . will all perish' (Luke 13:3). At Pentecost Peter said, 'Repent!' Paul declared that God has commanded all men everywhere to repent! (Acts 17:30). So what is repentance?

Repentance is *a radical change of mind* — radical in the sense that it involves a conversion, a turning about from travelling in one direction to take the opposite direction. Repentance is the prodigal actually getting on his feet and heading for home; it is a turning from Satan to God, from darkness to light. Without repentance there can be no salvation. On the Day of Pentecost it meant the recognition of the sin of deicide. Those who repented changed their minds about the Christ. Instead of vilifying him as they had done before, they now believed him to be the Son of God. Their repentance was publicly exhibited in baptism. Repentance is essential because you cannot continue in the devil's camp and claim to be a follower of Jesus at the same time.

Repentance is the *gift of God* (Acts 5:31; 11:18). It is a change of mind which turns a man from serving himself and his idols to serve the living God. Repentance is inseparable from faith. This connection of faith with repentance can be seen in the way the two are frequently joined together in the ministry of our Lord and the apostles: 'Repent and believe the good news!' (Mark 1:15); 'Repent, then, and turn to God' (Acts 3:19); 'Repent and be baptized' (Acts 2:38).

While repentance and faith are inseparable they are different and are to be distinguished the one from the other. To be turned about is essential, but we are not justified by repentance. It is faith that joins us to Christ. There is sorrow in repentance, but to be sorry about my sin may not necessarily turn me away from it. To repent is to have a decisive change of mind which results in action, but that action is not to be regarded as a merit which puts me in good standing with God. It is the receiving of Christ's righteousness alone which puts me in good standing with God. Some try to quantify faith and repentance. How much faith is needed? How much repentance? The answer is that a weak faith can take hold of a strong Christ, but faith, to be saving, must join the sinner to Christ. In revival there can be enormous emotional upheavals and deep churnings of soul. But the main point is that the ungodly life must be forsaken (repentance), and the new life of faith taken up. We must enter in by the narrow gate and walk along the narrow path. Yet again, we must take care never to add conditions. Christ alone saves and he will give his followers everything necessary for faithful discipleship. It is right to warn of the high cost of discipleship as Jesus did (Matt. 8:18-22). To believe may cost you your life, but the Lord is not saying, 'Be a good disciple first and then you will qualify for salvation.' You will never by your own merits qualify in any way for salvation. The fact that you are a lost and guilty sinner is your qualification to come in repentance for a complete pardon and the gift of a perfect salvation.

The new birth

The necessity of regeneration was very much to the fore in the eighteenth-century awakening. To say a man must be born again is another way of saying that he is hopelessly lost and depraved in all his faculties. It is impossible for a man to give himself new birth. Once Jesus had impressed this on Nicodemus, he held up the cross as the only solution: 'Just as Moses lifted up the snake in the desert, so the Son of Man must be lifted up, that everyone who believes in him may have eternal life' (John 3:14). The Methodists multiplied numerically through the First and Second Great Awakenings. Many of them, including John and Charles Wesley, were confused and in error about the doctrine of predestination, but in spite of that they were clear about man's lostness in sin and therefore the necessity of the new birth from heaven. They were insistent upon radical repentance. The easy-believism of our late twentieth century would have been entirely unacceptable to the Methodists. The reason for that is that although they were muddle-headed about the doctrine of the sovereignty of God, in their experience of revival they knew well what it was to be saved from sin and hell by the mighty power of God. Nevertheless, we should be clear about sovereign grace in our hearts as well as our heads, and it is to that theme we now turn.

4. Revival highlights the subject of sovereign grace

What is sovereign grace?

Picture the scene in Jerusalem. Here assembled were many of those who had rejected and murdered our Lord Jesus Christ. The heinous nature of their sin came home to their consciences with tremendous power by the Holy Spirit. Could there be forgiveness for them? When the people heard Peter's words about Jesus being made both Lord and Christ, 'they were cut to the heart' because Peter had reminded them that they had crucified this same Jesus. They called out to Peter and the other apostles, 'Brothers, what shall we do?' The instructions were clear: 'Peter replied, "Repent and be baptized, every one of you, in the name of Jesus Christ for the forgiveness of your sins. And you will receive the gift of the Holy Spirit."'

Note that there is a twofold promise made to those who repent: firstly, the forgiveness of sin, and secondly, the gift of the Holy Spirit. Central to the fulfilment of these promises is the preaching of Christ. The Christ who is held before them is the same one whom they had sought to put on the rubbish heap of history. But now Jahweh had exalted this Jesus to be the Lord of history. He whom they had so cruelly maligned now occupied the supreme place of honour and majesty over all the universe. It was up to him whether or not those who had spat upon him should be pardoned for their crime. It was not an automatic matter. Without the assurance of their acceptance given to them by the Holy Spirit, there could be no salvation for these criminals. God will have mercy upon whom he will have mercy and he will harden whom he will (Rom. 9:15-16). This is not to import an idea into the passage. Some of the unbelieving Jews were saved and others continued in impenitence. God's mercy alone made the difference. The Christ-hating Jews in

Jerusalem continued in their contempt of Christ and demonstrated their hellish hatred of him by stoning Stephen to death.

Those who appealed to Peter were instructed to repent. This meant that they had to change their minds completely about Jesus. They were also commanded to be baptized. The implications of baptism for them were the same as for converted Muslims today. It was costly because allegiance to the crucified Christ was regarded as treason. It was also costly because the Jews regarded baptism as necessary for Gentile converts only. By baptism these converts would demonstrate their submission to the very person whom they had previously rejected. For each one it meant passing through the agony of seeking mercy and pardon. The same Spirit who convinced them of their crime also convinced each one personal!), of forgiveness. What for most converts takes weeks, months and some-times years, was concentrated into hours. This intensification of the work of the Holy Spirit characterizes revival. For each repenting sinner there is the agony of conviction and seeking the mercy of God. This is aptly descibed in Zechariah 12:10: 'And I will pour out on the house of David and the inhabitants of Jerusalem a spirit of grace and supplication. They will look on me, the one they have pierced, and they will mourn for him as one mourns for an only child ... On that day the weeping in Jerusalem will be great.' This weeping was followed by great joy in reconciliation to Christ, and by him reconciliation to the Father. It was the joy of a free justification together with adoption into God's family.

It was the joy too of receiving the gift of the person and work of the Holy Spirit, the Comforter.

On the basis of the conversions of Pentecost (and all the conversions reported thereafter in the book of Acts) I would propose two-principles:

1. The work of preaching Christ in all his glory as Saviour and Lord and exhorting to faith and repentance belongs to the preacher.

2. The work of applying the gospel to the hearts and consciences of sinners, both in conviction and assurance, belongs to the Holy Spirit alone.

The degree to which a sinner is convicted, the depth of his repentance, the degree of his faith and the depth of assurance to which he is brought, is all the sovereign work of the Holy Spirit alone. The timing of this work also belongs to the Spirit. Peter and the apostles could not even begin to know which souls in Jerusalem would be converted that day. Before the event they had no idea how long such a work would take to achieve. Certainly nothing of this magnitude and speed had taken place under the ministry of Jesus on earth. This was a work of spiritual awakening directed by Jesus from his throne of supreme authority. In his earthly ministry, even after his sensational miracle of multiplying the loaves and fish to feed 5,000, the people were still in contention about him. More seemed to be leaving him than were coming to him (John 6:60-70).

The above two principles are highlighted by Pentecost. With all his heart Peter proclaimed the gospel. That work belonged to him and to the apostles. But the application of the gospel to the souls of those converted belonged entirely to the Holy Spirit. Only by him could any person that day experience assurance of salvation. The imparting of assurance is something entirely outside the ability of counsellors or advisers (Rom. 8:15-16; Gal. 4:6). A counsellor can advise and exhort and pray with a soul under deep conviction, but the experience of peace with God is the work of the Holy Spirit.

The truth of sovereign grace is illustrated by the vision of the valley of dry bones described in Ezekiel 37. Only the Spirit could bring the bones together, put flesh on them and raise them to life. To Ezekiel belonged the work of preaching and praying; to the Spirit, the work of raising the dead. This doctrine of sovereign grace is explained in Ephesians 2. When we were dead in sins God raised us up to be made alive 'in Christ'. Occasionally we come across Christians who have been converted suddenly through the unexpected powerful intervention of God. In most cases such believers do not struggle with the truth that salvation belongs to the Lord. Sovereign grace is ingrained in them.

In times of spiritual barrenness it is difficult to get sinners to see that they have any need at all. In a period of spiritual apathy, many ministers resort to manipulation in order to obtain visible results. The opposite is true in a time of powerful spiritual awakening.

Overcome by an awesome sense of the holiness of God, the problem for convicted sinners is to believe that there could actually be mercy and salvation for them. Then it is of paramount importance that Christ be clearly exhibited as the one in whom the believer has righteousness, holiness and redemption (1 Cor. 1:30).

5. Pentecost compared with the revival under David Brainerd

When revival came to the Indians among whom Brainerd had laboured long, with very little visible success, he described the intensity of conviction and repentance in his diary: 'It seemed to me there was now an exact fulfilment of that great prophecy, Zechariah 12:10-12, for there was now "a great mourning, like the mourning of Hadadrimmon", and each seemed to "mourn apart".' Brainerd thought this bore a close resemblance to the day of God's power, mentioned in Joshua 10:14: 'I must say I never saw any day like it in all respects. It was a day wherein I am persuaded the Lord did much to destroy the kingdom of darkness among his people... This was indeed a surprising day of God's power and seemed enough to convince an atheist of the truth, importance and power of God's word.'

The burdened and prayerful David Brainerd had faced fully the reality of what we call total depravity. He had witnessed a people completely lost in the darkness of unbelief and superstition, a people totally disinterested in the gospel. Only the drawing power of an omnipotent God could possibly disengage the Indians from their idolatry and change their natures. Now the floodgates of grace had opened and Brainerd had the joy of seeing the proof 'that the conversion of untutored, uncivilized men to Christianity, by the simple means of preaching, is not an impossible, nor a wild and imaginary thing. The gospel among bond and free, the civilized and barbarous, when accompanied with the Holy Ghost sent down from heaven, is the power of God to salvation.'

The news spread of the exciting events, so that some Indians came 'more than forty miles to hear the young white preacher, but many came without an inkling of what was taking place'. 'Many came without any intelligence of what was going on here,' he reports, 'and consequently without any design of theirs . . . so that it seemed as if God had summoned them together from all quarters for nothing else but to deliver his message to them.' The news had spread also into the white villages so that 'Numbers of careless spectators of the white people came and were awakened and could no longer be idle spectators.' The work continued with varying degrees of intensity, so that on 16 August *1745* he could comment, 'I never saw the work of God appear so independent of means as at this time ... God's manner of working upon them appeared so entirely supernatural and above means that I could scarcely believe he used me as an instrument, or what I spake as means of carrying on his work ... Although I could not but continue to use the means which I thought proper for the promotion of the work, yet God seemed, as I apprehended, to work entirely without them. I seemed to do nothing, and indeed to have nothing to do, but to "stand still and see the salvation of God" ... God appeared to work entirely alone, and I saw no room to attribute any part of this work to any created arm.'

How long did this moving of God last? What were the consequences of it? On 28 October he reports, 'The Word of God seemed to fall on the assembly with a divine power and influence, especially toward the end of my discourse ... so much of the divine presence appeared in the assembly that it seemed "This was no other than the house of God, and the gate of heaven ..." If ever there was among my people an appearance of the New Jerusalem — "as a bride adorned for her husband" — there was much at this time.' Or, moving to Sunday 15 December, 'This was an amazing season of grace! The word of the Lord this day "was quick and powerful, sharper than a two-edged sword" and pierced to the hearts of many. The assembly was greatly affected and deeply wrought upon ... Oh how the hearts of the hearers seemed to bow under the weight of divine truths! And how evident did it appear that they received and felt them "not as the word of man, but as the word of God"'. Again, on Christmas day, 'The power attending divine truths seemed to have the influence of the earthquake, rather than of the whirlwind upon them.' On the last day of 1745 Brainerd reported that he returned to his house: 'They soon came in one after another with tears in their eyes to know what they should do to be saved. And the divine Spirit in such a manner fastened upon their hearts what I spoke to them, that the house was soon filled with cries and groans — a season of great power amongst them; it seemed as if God had bowed the heavens and come down— and I was ready to think then, that I should never again despair of the conversion of any man or woman living, be they who or what they would.'

Three months later, in reviewing the situation, Brainerd wrote,

I know of no assembly of Christians where there seems to be so much of the presence of God, where brotherly love so much prevails, and where I should take so much delight in the public worship of God in general as in my own congregation; although nine months ago they were worshipping devils and idols under the power of pagan darkness and superstition. Amazing change this! Affected by nothing less than divine power and grace! This is the Lord's doing and marvellous in our eyes!

If we compare the character of this revival with Pentecost we should see the similarity. We see it in the agonizing intercession and struggle which preceded the revival. We see it too in the intensity and swiftness of the work of the Spirit when he did come in awakening power. We see it in the content of what was preached. Brainerd preached Christ from the Old Testament and the New. He was especially fond of Isaiah. He exposed the dreadful results of the fall of mankind into sin. It is clear that the Indians believed absolutely in the reality of hell as an outcome of his preaching. Brainerd was an expert in displaying the all-sufficiency of Christ, his life, his death and, especially, his power now to save to the uttermost all that come to God through him. He preached the full and free offers of the gospel without inhibition of any kind. For every destitute sinner flying to Christ for refuge there would be found salvation and all needed grace. Brainerd went straight to the issue that the heart of man is fallen, corrupt and at enmity with God. He declared that only regeneration could change that. He discouraged commotion and swooning. He was satisfied only with a work that bore the marks of the Holy Spirit in a rational yet heartfelt turning to, and resting in, Christ. Before his early death, aged twenty-nine, Brainerd was given great liberty in praying for the advancement of Christ's kingdom on earth. To that end he longed that the Holy Spirit should descend on and rest on preachers, enabling them to address the consciences of men with closeness and power.[3]

The revival among the Indians just described is similar to many other revivals that have been documented. The question is, are these revivals in essence adequate to meet the needs of the peoples of the world as we find it today? Is the gospel prospered by the Holy Spirit in the manner just described adequate, or do we have to search for new and additional dimensions? I would suggest that we have all we need in the gospel of Christ. If we preach him with the power of the Holy Spirit sent down from heaven in spiritual awakening, that is sufficient to conquer the forces of the world, of sin and darkness and of Satan.

*Reasons for
Specific Prayer for
Revival*

5. The biblical doctrine of repentance demands it

Repentance and revival are brought together in 2 Chronicles 7:14: 'If my people, who are called by my name, will humble themselves and pray and seek my face and turn from their wicked ways, then will I hear from heaven and will forgive their sin and will heal their land.'

We need to observe the following principles.

First, there is always a people who by their allegiance to the Scriptures and by their holy lives fit the description, 'my people ... called by my name'. The name of God is used in such a way as to imply everything that he has revealed about himself to the prophets, as recorded in Holy Scripture.

Secondly, when the cause of the 'people called by my name' — represented by the Jews in the Old Testament epoch — and by the Christian church in our dispensation — when their cause is barren, then a way to healing and restoration is suggested — namely, corporate repentance. When we speak of 'the church' we mean by that the sum of all those churches where the gospel is preached. There are now many denominations. The mainline denominations are mixed in character. Each individual church has to be tested with what have been called 'the marks of a true church'. Faithful preaching of the gospel is the first mark of a true church. How can evangelical churches express repentance in a united way when they are so fragmented? An encouraging step in this direction has been the formation of regional fraternals for evangelical pastors in many parts of Britain, in which those from different denominations meet together at regular intervals.

The corporate repentance spoken of in 2 Chronicles 7:14 consists of four elements: God's people are to humble themselves, seek his face, pray and turn from their wicked ways.

1. The call to humble ourselves

Isaiah stresses that the Almighty One lives with the humble. It is especially the humble whom the Lord revives. This is an abiding principle which we see in Isaiah 57:15:

> For this is what the high and lofty One says —
>> he who lives for ever, whose name is holy:
> I live in a high and holy place,
>> but also with him who is contrite and lowly in spirit,
> to revive the spirit of the lowly
>> and to revive the heart of the contrite.

Humility includes the confession of our poverty and need. In prayer for revival we should confess our sorrow for the spiritual deadness which afflicts the churches and for the indifference which characterizes the people among whom we live.

To humble ourselves means that we repent sincerely of the poverty of our relationship with the Lord. Repentance is not just an initial act; it is ongoing. It is something which we always need to renew.

It is wonderful to observe that repentance is attractive to God. The Bible as a whole proclaims that repentance and faith is the way of reconciliation with God. The message of the apostles is summed up in this, that they preached 'repentance toward God and faith in the Lord Jesus Christ'. Repentance is a work of the Holy Spirit in the hearts of men to bring them to a change of mind (Acts 5:31; 11:18). Why is repentance attractive to God? The answer surely must be that repentance stands at the threshhold of a restored relationship. Repentance is to life (Acts 11:18), that is, it is a turning from Satan to God, from darkness to light, from the wages of death to union with Christ, who is the source of life eternal. Jesus' teaching on repentance is more clearly portrayed in Luke 15 than anywhere else. He shows in a variety of ways that repentance is most precious in character. It is the finding of the lost coin, the bringing home of the lost sheep, the return to the Father of the prodigal son. The angels in heaven rejoice over one sinner who repents. To the amazement of the neighbours, who are disgusted with the bad record of the prodigal, the father runs out of the town to embrace his son and bring him home. The father then calls for a joyful banquet, for this his son was dead but is alive again. The older brother in the parable shows that he urgently stands in need of heart repentance because his affections are far from his father and his attitude is far from right.

2. The call to seek God's face

This I take to be a reference to special prayer. Jonathan Edwards referred to prayer meetings held in addition to the regular weekly ones as 'extraordinary prayer'. At such times churches may come together for days of fasting and prayer for revival and awakening.

In the concluding chapter I suggest ways in which such prayer meetings may be conducted, so at this point I will simply refer to one of the foremost features suggested by the words, 'Seek my face'. In both personal and corporate prayers it is vital to seek the face of the Lord. That I take to be a reference to the assurance of face-to-face dealing, the presence of the triune God felt in our souls.

If we were promised an audience with an earthly monarch we would not be content merely to see a representative in the foyer. We would expect to see the monarch face to face and to be able to communicate verbally with him or her. This illustrates the point that in our prayers we are not simply sending in requests. We are seeking God's face in our affections and require assurance in our souls that we are indeed in his presence and are being heard by him. We must pray 'in the Spirit' (Eph. 6:18) on all occasions, but especially when we are calling on him to come and heal our land and to return to us again in power. Surely that power will first be felt in our own souls!

3. The call to prayer

In the context, specific prayer is referred to, that is intercession that God will heal the land, which has been subject to drought, famine or plague. The nature of the judgement is specific and therefore the nature of the intercession for relief and deliverance must be specific. In our generation we have increasingly suffered from powerlessness and spiritual lethargy. More and more our churches have been subject to spiritual weakness and their impact upon the world has, with all too few exceptions, been minimal. In many instances a great deal of outreach has been attempted with pitifully little, or nothing, to show for it. In most cases the proportion of believers to unbelievers is on the decline.

Prayer, then, needs to be specific. In *The Welsh Revival*, a description is given of the special and specific prayer which preceded the 1859 revival in Wales (not the 1904 Welsh revival referred to previously). The extent to which prayer was resorted to in that instance is very striking.

The description runs as follows:

The Lord has caused his people to feel more deeply than ever the need of a gracious revival, not only in the world, but also in the church; and this feeling has found expression in prayer, more generally and more intensely than at any former period within our memory. In the closet, at the family altar, and in the public congregation, this great blessing has been sought with persevering earnestness. Even in prayer it has been found that union is strength. In numerous instances Christian congregations, in addition to the usual or special gathering for prayer in their own sanctuaries, have united with others for this high and holy purpose in some public room, or alternately in their several places of worship.

Meetings for prayer have been held in all sorts of places, and attended by all sorts of people. In churches and chapels, in vestries and school-rooms, in town halls and market places, in the covered tent and in the open field, in the recesses of the forest and on mountain top, in the saloons of steamers, and on the open decks of sailing vessels — meetings for special prayer have been held; and in some instances, elegant drawing rooms have been thrown open for this purpose, while, on a late memorable occasion, the Egyptian Hall of the Mansion House was converted for a time into a Christian oratory. In all these places, from the lips and hearts of the thousands who attended them, one prayer has ascended up before God's throne: ' O Lord, revive thy work in the midst of the years.' 'Wilt thou not revive us again, that thy people may rejoice in thee?'

And the blessing, thus ardently and generally sought, has been graciously vouchsafed. Verily there is a God who hears and answers prayer. The Christian Church has been greatly revived in this and other lands. While the kingdom of darkness has been sensibly shaken, multitudes have been made to feel that religion is indeed a reality. The Revival, so called, is one of the great topics of the day. No section of the community is able to ignore it. The pulpit, the platform and the press all unite to proclaim the wonderful religious movement of the times in which we live.

'America was the first to wake up from her awful spiritual torpor; and it is said that no fewer than six hundred thousand persons in the United States have, within the last two years, been led to make a profession of religion.

England has not been wholly forgotten; for although we cannot yet speak of any great and overwhelming movement in any one locality, yet in many places, both in the metropolis and elsewhere, "the Spirit of God is moving upon the face of the waters" and now and again makes his presence felt, by mighty operations upon the hearts and consciences of sinners.

'Scotland has been visited with a gracious shower, as the accounts from Glasgow, Edinburgh, Aberdeen and many other places testify.

Ireland also is now thoroughly awake, rising out of the dust, and putting on her beautiful garments. Sweden likewise is experiencing a powerful and widespread revival, chiefly as the result of Scripture circulation and the evangelistic efforts of those who have themselves known by experience the power of the truth.

And lastly, to return to the principality of Wales, by no means a stranger to revivals in years gone by, she has also in these days been blessed with an abundant outpouring of 'the latter rain'.[1]

4. The call to turn from our wicked ways

It is wicked to steal and to slander. It is wicked to indulge in drunkenness and adultery. It is wicked to neglect parents or to be cruel to children. It is also wicked to rob God of the love we owe him, when he has shown his love for us by giving his all for us in the form of his eternally begotten Son.

Lukewarmness in the church at Laodicea was not regarded as a matter of minor importance; it was the most offensive sin in that church. Likewise we note the severity of our Lord's words to the church at Ephesus which had been commended in so many ways. He actually describes them as a fallen church and threatens them with demise: 'Yet I hold this against you: You have forsaken your first love. Remember the height from which you have fallen! Repent and do the things you did at first. If you do not repent, I will come to you and remove your lampstand from its place' (Rev. 2:5).

In our secular society incipient spiritual decline is always going on. Many come to regard their favourite TV programmes as more important than the prayer meeting. Obviously if we are to be earnest in our quest for revival we will get nowhere while we are not prepared to turn from our wicked ways. A Reformed pastor in America was discouraged to discover that when one of the Lord's Day services clashed with a major baseball fixture, 160 of his normal congregation opted to stay at home and watch the match on TV, while a mere forty attended the service. It is also common in other countries to find Christians showing much greater affection for a sport than for the gospel. When does a lawful hobby become idolatry? Surely the answer is, when we show more enthusiasm for our hobbies than we do for the ordinances of God.

Like Daniel, Ezra and Nehemiah, we should identify ourselves with the sins of the nation of which we form a part. Are we not to blame corporately as the church for our compromise and the fact that affairs have reached so low an ebb?

Should we not repent on behalf of the society in which we live? Is that not the way to turn from our wicked ways? It is hypocritical to lament the sad state of those around us whose lives have been wrecked by sin while regarding ourselves as superior. Rather, we should realize that we too would have been wrecked but for the grace of God.

Repentance includes a willingness to accept the physical discipline of prayer, which may sometimes include fasting. Our first efforts at departing from our lethargy and laziness may be weak and feeble but a start is made. We are proceeding along the right lines especially when we confess our sad spiritual condition. An athlete who has allowed himself to get badly out of condition cannot expect to compete satisfactorily in that state, but he can determine forthwith to begin to work on a programme which will gradually bring him back to fitness. Repentance in the heart is required to be immediate and sincere, but clearly hard work over a period of time is needed to correct bad habits and replace them with healthy ones. One immediate step indicating sincerity in repentance is to abandon a favourite TV programme which keeps the believer at home instead of attending the weekly prayer meeting.

That weekly meeting might be well below what it ought to be, butoften the beginning of a time of revival has been the quickening of the ordinary prayer meetings, resulting in new vitality, more participation, more sense of the presence of the Holy Spirit, more unction in intercession, more burden and a greater willingness to promote evangelism and the Lord's work.

A principal problem in our Western society is that Christians are over-indulgent in lawful pleasures. Many pursuits are lawful: gardening, hiking, golf, good food, holidays, attractive homes and smart clothes are all lawful; but when any combination of lawful pursuits join hands to absorb most of the zeal and time of professing believers, the result is an ineffectual and lukewarm church. A small minority of zealous Christians are left to wear themselves out in carrying the whole load.

'If my people ... will pray and ... turn from their wicked ways, then will I hear from heaven and will forgive their sin and will heal their land' (2 Chr. 7:14).

6. The history of the church dictates it

In his book *A History of the Work of Redemption*, Jonathan Edwards made this observation: 'It may be observed that from the fall of man to our day, the work of redemption in its effect has mainly been carried on by remarkable pourings out of the Spirit of God.'

We must be careful not to overstate this principle. It is noteworthy that Edwards himself immediately goes on to qualify this assertion by saying, 'Though there be a more constant influence of God's Spirit always in some degree attending his ordinances, yet the way in which the greatest things have been done in carrying on this work always has been by remarkable pourings out of the Spirit at special seasons of mercy.'

Is Edwards correct in making the above claims? A major problem besets the student of revival as he surveys the history of redemption, and that is the difference between the Old Testament era and our own. Writers like Richard Owen Roberts and Dr Robert Lescelius tend to assume that revivals in Old Testament times were the same in nature and kind as those we have on record in recent history, such as the Great Awakening of the eighteenth century.

For instance, Richard Owen Roberts lists twelve revivals in the Old Testament as follows:

1. The revival under Moses	Exodus 32ff.
2. The revival under Samuel	1 Samuel 7 (with chapters 1-6 providing the background).
3. The revival under David	2 Samuel 6-7.

4. The revival under Asa   2 Chronicles 14-16.
5. The revival under Jehoshaphat   2 Chronicles 17-20.
6. The revival under Jehoiada   2 Chronicles 23-24.
7. The revival under Hezekiah   2 Chronicles 29-32.
8. The revival under Josiah   2 Chronicles 34-35.
9. The revival under Zerubbabel   Ezra 1-6.
10. The revival under Ezra   Ezra 7-10.
11. The revival under Nehemiah   Nehemiah 1-13.
12. The revival under Joel   Joel 2:12-27.[1]

Roberts brings out the place of the 'solemn assembly' which is extremely practical and valuable. Having carefully studied the passages listed above, I do not believe that all the instances referred to were revivals. We simply do not have enough information to establish such a claim. The kings mentioned sought to bring reformation and purification, but to what extent genuine repentance swept the nation is difficult to say. Certainly Isaiah has nothing to say about the reformation or revival that is claimed for Hezekiah. It is clear that there was at least outwardly an extensive attempt at national reformation, but Isaiah's silence is a caution against claiming too much. Likewise Jeremiah is consistently pessimistic about the state of the nation of Judah. This pessimism was justified by the horrific events of the ultimate fall and destruction of Jerusalem. Jeremiah never refers to the reformation promoted by Josiah. Whatever was accomplished it certainly was not enough to avert the severe judgement that came in the time of Jeremiah. In revival, as we understand it, there would have been repentance on a large scale which would have averted judgement of God's people.

In similar fashion Robert Lescelius takes 2 Chronicles and suggests that there was revival under the kings Rehoboam, Asa, Jehoshaphat, Hezekiah and Josiah.[2] The nearest thing to a Holy Spirit revival as we understand it today would seem to have taken place under King Asa and later under King Hezekiah.

Three chapters in 2 Chronicles are devoted to the reign of King Asa and mostly describe the king's own experiences. However, we do have this description of the people and their zeal to follow the Lord: 'They entered into a covenant to seek the Lord, the God of their fathers, with all their heart and soul. All who would not seek the Lord, the God of Israel, were to be put to death, whether small or great, man or woman. They took an oath to the Lord with loud acclamation, with shouting and with trumpets and horns. All Judah rejoiced about the oath because they had sworn it whole-heartedly. They sought God eagerly, and he was found by them. So the Lord gave them rest on every side' (2 Chron. 15:12-15). We would hardly impose the death penalty upon those not willing to be revived today!

In his book on revival Brian Edwards majors on Hezekiah as an example of revival.[3] Elements of revival are present, but overall what was accomplished under Hezekiah is surely better described as a reformation.

Biblical theology is the framework for Old Testament study

As we make a study of revival we need to recognize that biblical theology (progressive revelation) is the predominant principle undergirding our understanding of the history of redemption. It is misguided to think that revival is the key to understanding the Old Testament. Revival is not the key. The key is that God was revealing himself progressively and systematically and what we have now in the Bible is the outcome of that work of progressive revelation. The study of revival must be subservient to this principle. The Old Testament era was a time of divine interventions. Stage by stage Yahweh intervened in human affairs. First he formed a family under Abraham; then he formed a nation from Abraham's offspring. Once that was established, he intervened time and again, either to preserve his people or to move them forward to a new stage of progress or understanding, all the while preparing for the incarnation and the ushering in of the New Testament age. One major plateau was reached, and then another, not so much by revival as by direct intervention and revelation of his Word. Once established in the land of Israel, the nation was initially sustained more by military exploits than by revivals in the sense that we know them today. In the prophetic age ushered in by Samuel and David, reformation was dominant. As I have suggested, it is difficult to pinpoint clearly the incidence of revivals in that epoch in the way that we understand revival now.

The instances in the Old Testament which seem to come nearest to the New Testament portrayal of revival, with deep repentance and turning to God, are at Bokim and under Nehemiah.

The preaching of our Lord by theophany at Bokim, reported in Judges 2:1-4, stirred the people: 'When the angel of the Lord had spoken these things to all the Israelites, the people wept aloud.'

Likewise under Nehemiah the great assembly of hearers were broken in heart as they listened to the book of the Law being read and expounded to them. Ezra said, '"This day is sacred to the Lord your God. Do not mourn or weep." For all the people had been weeping as they listened to the words of the Law' (Neh. 8:9).

Interventions of God

The interventions of God in the Old Testament provide us with a great incentive to pray for revival. As we trace out these interventions we see that God's purpose is being fulfilled stage by stage. 'From him and through him and to him are all things' (Rom. 11:36). The glory of our triune God is the supreme purpose of human history. Apparently arbitrary and confusing events of one period make sense when looked at in the light of later history. For instance, when the children of God went into captivity it was for them an experience of excruciating pain and humiliation. With hindsight we can see why it had to be so. Jonathan Edwards speaks of God's subordinate purposes and his ultimate purpose. He subordinates human affairs and developments in such a way as to serve his ultimate purpose, which is to establish his kingdom and glorify his Son. It is this ultimate purpose which fills us with confidence that, with regard to the spiritual conquest of this world, the crown of victory will not be placed on the serpent's head but on the head of the Lamb. We should observe the striking way in which God intervened over and over again in the Old Testament epoch. Revivals are God's interventions in this last time. What is revival if it is not the intervention of God in human affairs on a grand scale in great power and glory?

We will glance now at three major interventions in Israel's history: the Exodus, the raising up of Samuel, and the return from Babylon. In each case there is substantial instruction and encouragement for us with regard to the subject of revival.

1. The intervention of the Exodus

In the case of the Exodus the condition of Israel under the Egyptian taskmasters and the dominion of Pharaoh was pitiful. The Lord assured Moses at the burning bush that he had heard the groans of his people, the covenant children of Abraham, Isaac and Jacob. Such was the servility of the people, and the power of Pharaoh to control them and use them for his own ends, that Moses was totally disenchanted with the idea of going back and confronting so awesome a power. Let the Lord find someone else. Moses would rather look after sheep in the wilderness than hazard his life and energies on a risky and ridiculous escapade. The Lord became irked by Moses' intransigence and insisted that he would have to do what he was told.

If you did not know the story, would you conceive of a million people escaping intact from slavery? 'God moves in a mysterious way his wonders to perform.' We take encouragement from the fact that the groans of the Israelites were heard. Prayer is the principal means of grace to be employed by the Lord's people. The whole nation came out of Egypt with all their livestock and with their needs supplied. It was the beginning of a new era. We should entertain no doubt about the omnipotence of God, nor ever think he may be short in knowledge and wisdom as to how he can change the face of society.

2. The prayers of Hannah and the reformation under Samuel

'Who despises the day of small things?' (Zech. 4:10). Who would make much of a woman fasting, praying and weeping because of childlessness? Yet Hannah, the mother of Samuel, marks the commencement of the next epoch in Israel's history. The period of the judges was awful. How could that be changed? The change came through Hannah's burden and her dedication. When the

Lord answered her petition and gave her a son she called him Samuel and gave him to the Lord for the whole of his life (1 Sam. 1:28). Samuel taught Israel on circuit, going from centre to centre — Bethel, Gilgal, Mizpeh. He became the first in a line of a new succession of prophets (Acts 3:24). We read that under Samuel's ministry, 'All the people of Israel mourned and sought after the Lord' (1 Sam. 7:2).

Rather than undervaluing the place of prayer, let us see what a great privilege it is. We come to the throne of grace and power (Heb. 4:14-16). Who would think that the start of a new epoch would be marked by the prayers of an unhappy woman?

3. The prayers of Daniel and the return from Babylon

Daniel was about fourteen years old when he was taken into Babylon as a captive together with about 10,000 others. Seven decades later he was studying the writings of the prophet Jeremiah and read the prediction that the desolation of Jerusalem would last seventy years (Jer. 29:10-14). Part of this prophecy of restoration concerns the prayers that would accompany that time of return: 'This is what the Lord says: "When seventy years are completed for Babylon, I will come to you and fulfil my gracious promise to bring you back to this place" '(Jer. 29:10-13).

Far from viewing the fulfilment of the promise as an inevitability, Daniel set himself to intercede with the utmost fervour, fasting in sackcloth and ashes (Dan. 9:1-3). Daniel's prayer is one of the great prayers of the Bible. It is full of humility and specific confession of sin but also powerful pleading of the promise that had been made.

In Daniel's intercession we have a model as to how we should set about prayer for revivals and awakenings. He sets an example of locating the specific promise and pleading its fulfilment. It is true that the promises made for the furtherance of the gospel to the ends of the earth are general, but there is the specific promise of spiritual awakening among the Jews which we should plead with the same fervour as Daniel pleaded for restoration.

Revival and the progress of the church in this dispensation

We should not overlook the fact that the sudden appearance of John the Baptist in the wilderness preaching with magnetic power had all the characteristics of an awakening. Especially noteworthy is the call to repentance and the way in which large numbers travelled a long way to hear preaching which did not flatter them but went straight to the heart.

The book of Acts is a description of the revivals which followed Pentecost. Many churches were established. For instance, the church at Corinth came into being through a most powerful revival. How many churches in the West today can point to converted homosexuals, drunkards, swindlers, thieves, idolaters and prostitutes? (1 Cor. 6:9-11).

The long period from the time of Constantine to the sixteenth-century Reformation is one of decline. Relatively little work has been done to evaluate the extent to which the work of such men as Columba, Peter of Bruys, Arnold of Brescia, Peter Waldo, Savanarola, Wycliffe, Jan Hus and Jerome would, or could, be regarded as revival. Certainly if the feature of large numbers being turned to faith is to be regarded as a criteria then these leaders should be viewed as instruments of revival.

I will comment in more detail on the Waldensians, who were disciples of Peter Waldo, and in addition refer to the pre-Reformation movement known as the *Devotio Moderna*.

In about 1170 in Lyons, France, there lived a wealthy merchant by name, Peter Waldo. He employed a priest to translate the Gospels into French. Waldo himself embraced the gospel and then trained other believers to go two by two into the whole of southern France preaching the gospel. Those who believed were gathered into groups. Waldo made sure that parts of the Bible were provided for them. This movement spread through southern France, into Switzerland and northern Italy.

As the Waldensians increased cruel persecution came from the Roman Catholic Church. Some fled to other nations, while many took refuge in the Piedmont mountains. Even there they were hounded to death. At one time 400 women and children were housed in a cave while the men were away. When this was discovered by their enemies, a fire was lit in the entrance to the cave and all those inside perished. In his day, Oliver Cromwell did all he could to relieve the suffering of the Waldensians. Although few in number now, they have survived in Italy to the present time.

We must not entertain romanticized ideas about the believers of the pre-Reformation period. Deprived of sound teaching materials, it is not surprising that they were confused on a number of issues. Nevertheless they made the most of what they had and their courage and devotion put us, who have so many advantages which they did not have, to shame.

The *Devotio Moderna*, (meaning the modern style of devotion), was by far the most important of many reform movements prior to the Reformation.[4] It began in Holland through a Dutchman, Gerhard Groote (1340 - 1384). A son of wealthy parents, he was wild as a youth, but after his conversion, he gathered round him a group of dedicated disciples who became the nucleus from which an extensive movement grew. This movement soon produced men of sterling leadership ability. Groote worked hard to translate portions of the Scripture into the vernacular and to provide hymns so that the believers would have adequate spiritual resources. He came into conflict with the church. However, it was the time of the papal schism and by appealing to Pope Urban VI, he survived.

John Cele and Alexander Hegius were men of great talent who furthered the cause of the Brethren of the Common Life. Under John Cele's direction a school at Zwolle was established which attracted as many as 1200 students at one time.[5] Cele, like Groote before him, emphasized prayer and systematic Bible study.

Who can tell to what extent fervent prayer preceded the momentous sixteenth-century Reformation? When the Reformation came, most of those in the *Devotio Moderna* became its supporters. But was the Reformation itself a revival? We will consider that now.

The Reformation

The Reformation was so much a struggle out of the cocoon of medieval darkness and superstition, and so much a locked battle between the truth and error, that we tend to overlook the effect of the gospel on multitudes of people who were turned from darkness to light. Without those newly born believers the Reformation movement could never have survived. To illustrate this I will make reference to Luther's ministry at Wittenberg University, where he functioned as a tutor from 1512 until his death in 1546. What took place in the spiritual realm in that university faculty reflects the fact that an extensive outpouring of the Holy Spirit characterized the Reformation.

Once Luther's soul had been filled with the joy of justification by faith he did all in his power to persuade the faculty and students. They all appeared to belong to the medieval school, yet one by one they were won over to the Reformation. Some of his colleagues were men of crucial influence. For instance, George Spalatin, who had organized the university library in 1512, was adviser to the Elector

Frederick the Wise. John Lang, Luther's Greek tutor, was won over. There was no significant problem that Luther did not share and discuss with his intimate friends, and once their souls had been set on fire for the gospel they did all they could to further the Reformation. Lifelong friends who stood by him through all his trials, such as Nicholas von Amsdorf, came early to the truth. Once the entire faculty of twenty-two professors had been won over it was possible to strengthen the university to the point where it became the most telling force for the gospel in Europe. Thus it was that the most brilliant linguist of all, Philip Melanchthon (1497-1560), a child prodigy whose scholarly output began when he was only seventeen, joined the faculty at Wittenburg in 1518 to be professor of Greek at the age of twenty-one. Melanchthon, though not in the same league as Luther as a Reformer, was to render invaluable lifelong service to the cause. An average of about 200 students enrolled during the years up to 1516. About 400 students used to attend Luther's lectures.[6]

This was not an isolated instance. Peter Martyr was a converted monk from Naples. Such was the preaching of Martyr that every monk in a large monastery south of Pisa was converted, and the same applied in another monastic institution.[7] Martyr was also used to establish two substantial evangelical churches in Italy, both of which were subsequently persecuted out of existence by the Counter-Reformation.

When we come to consider John Calvin we ought to remember most of all that he was engaged in the evangelization of France. Pastors were trained intensely at Geneva and only when fully equipped were they sent into France. These pastors were tested in theology, in moral fibre and pastoral ability before they were recommended for this work. One contemporary estimated that in 1561 audiences of over a thousand attended Calvin's lectures every day.

Sending church-planters into France was a dangerous business. In due time many who went were martyred. For instance, in Rouen in 1562 Augustin Mariorat was sentenced to death for his preaching and publicly hanged. His head was then fixed to a pike and displayed at the town bridge as a means to deter others from embracing the gospel. Mariorat's sole crime was his preaching. After suffering mockery in an exhausting procession through the streets, his main concern was to exhort two companions in death to hold firm.

Mariorat was one of eighty-eight ministers officially dispatched into France by the Geneva Company of Pastors after long years of study and preparation. He had been most effective as a church-planter.

Indeed, such was the blessing that followed the preaching of these gospel messengers that after just a few years an official census in 1562 revealed that there were 2,150 churches with 3,000,000 members out of a total population of 20,000,000.[8]

The Puritans and subsequent revivals in England

The English Puritans developed the doctrines of sanctification, assurance and allied truths in practical and experimental terms to a higher degree than any other body of theologians. They were not noted for developing a theology of revival in the way that Jonathan Edwards expounded that theme. During a long period, commencing with the start of Elizabeth's reign in 1558, they experienced a rising tide of spiritual blessing. The extent to which the Puritan movement was a revival has yet to be assessed by historians. It is an intriguing subject. Examples of great increase can be cited, such as those under Samuel Fairclough of Kedington (1594-1677), or Richard Baxter of Kidderminster (1615-1691). Subsequently, from about 1662 on-wards, a time of decline affected England as a whole. Towards the end of his life John Owen commented on the outgoing tide of true religion but confidently expressed his faith that in due time the Lord would again revive his work.

And so it was, for the eighteenth-century saw the Great Awakening followed by an even more extensive work of the Holy Spirit from 1790 to 1840, the Second Great Awakening. In turn the Third Great Awakening took place in the years following 1859, and there was revival in Wales in 1904. Early on in 1824 a remarkable awakening came to the Hebrides of Scotland and there have been many recurrences in those parts right up to 1970.[9]

We have observed that the church has been revived and enlarged by outpourings of the Spirit from age to age. Each time the challenge confronting God's people has been different. We face new and varied perplexities today and unbelief of a daunting kind. But the revivals of the past teach us that he that sits in the heavens laughs at opposition. He has given to his Son the highest place of authority and power. He will reign at God's right hand until his enemies become his footstool. We are therefore to go out into the world with confidence, praying that the uttermost parts of the earth will become his possession.

7. The example of our predecessors encourages it

Pentecost, which was the first Christian revival, was preceded by ten days of intense prayer characterized by wholehearted unity. That principle of prayer is surely a model for us to follow. Not that we should mimic exactly the same procedure, because Pentecost was unique, representing the coming of the Holy Spirit to the church in a way that cannot be repeated. I am simply pointing to the principle as a reminder of the fact that prayer occupies a primary place in the advance of all the Lord's work, and especially so in the quest for revival.

It is not difficult to prove that prevailing prayer has commonly preceded revivals in the history of the church, although there have been exceptions, when the Spirit has come suddenly without any known preparation of prayer, rather along the lines suggested in Isaiah 59:16:

> He saw that there was no one,
> he was appalled that there was no one to intervene;
> so his own arm worked salvation for him.

Sometimes prayer is sustained over a period of years but at other times the answer is almost instant. A striking example of extraordinary prayer for revival resulting in a swift response is recorded in South African history. The Dutch Reformed Church in South Africa was well informed concerning the 1859 revival in the USA, Britain and other parts of Europe. There was a sense of grief and disappointment that South Africa had been bypassed. Special prayer meetings were convened for humble repentance and intercession for revival. During those prayer meetings the Holy Spirit came down in a phenomenal way like a mighty rushing wind. Church after church experienced this same phenomenon while they were at prayer. The phenomenon was not sought, or even thought about, and no other supernatural phenomena characterized the revival which followed a revival as powerful in all its ramifications as the preceding revivals overseas. God's people were revived, the unconverted were awakened and expansive missionary outreach ensued.[1]

Would it not be overwhelmingly gracious if the Lord came to revive us speedily, rather than leaving us, as we deserve, to languish for even longer than we have done? An earlier example of an immediate answer to such prayer comes from Vermont, USA, in 1816. An association of churches had agreed on a day to be set apart for prayer and fasting to seek revival. Forty churches were involved. Within the next twelve months, more than 866 were added to the churches of that association. In the same period, following that day of prayer and fasting, over 6,000 were added to the churches in Vermont as a whole, for the revival was not confined to the association, but compassed other denominations as well.[2]

The above instance belongs to an epoch which Paul Cook, in a paper on the subject at the Carey Conference 1990, described as 'the Forgotten Revival'. That is, it has been forgotten by those writers on revival who have used the term 'the First Great Awakening' of the Methodist revival from 1745 onwards and then described the 1859 Revival of the last century as 'the Second Great Awakening'. It is strange that, in general, American writers have been more aware of the continual and extensive revivals in Britain between 1790 and 1840. The reason is that the records here have been inaccessible, being mainly housed in the libraries of denominations where there is now no interest in past revivals. When examined, these annals reveal the revivals of this period to have been more widespread than those of the better known awakenings. In many parts of Britain, and especially in Cornwall, the power of God was manifested in such measure as to have few equals in church history.

Prevailing prayer preceded this epoch of revival which commenced at that time. The example of the Lord's people of that day can provide a tremendous inspiration for us.

The origin of the concert for prayer

The concept of a concert for prayer for revival was promoted by Jonathan Edwards, but the idea did not originate with him. The word 'concert' aptly explains what is involved. The skill of an orchestra lies in the ability of the musicians to harmonize in unison. It only takes one, playing his own piece in disregard of the rest, to ruin the performance. In a concert for prayer, there is agreement by ministers and often by the assemblies they lead, to pray in unison at specific times for the outpouring of the Holy Spirit in revival.

In October 1744 a number of ministers in Scotland covenanted to unite in prayer that God would 'revive true religion in all parts of Christendom ... and fill the whole earth with his glory'. They pledged to endeavour to persuade others to join with them. The arrangement made was to be binding for two years. Time was to be set aside weekly, either on Saturday evenings or Sunday mornings, so that Christians would be enlivened and encouraged in the awareness that so many throughout the Christian world were uniting in the same holy exercise, in praying societies, public meetings or alone in secret. Longer times of prayer were engaged in on specific days quarterly. Robe, in the preface to his *Sermons says*, 'This concert was first set on foot, spread, and carried on, without printing anything about it for some time, in the way of private, friendly correspondence, by letters in 1744.'[3]

At the end of the two years, several Scottish ministers printed and distributed a memorial, dated 26 August 1746, inviting still more to prayer. The new proposal was that the concert for prayer should be renewed, this time for seven years. 500 copies of the memorial were sent to New England.

On 12 January 1748, after first preaching a series of sermons to his people in favour of the practice, Jonathan Edwards published a treatise with the title *An Humble Attempt to Promote Explicit agreement and Visible Union of God's People in extraordinary*

Prayer for the Revival of Religion and the Advancement of Christ's Kingdom on Earth. Lengthy as this title is, it is an abbreviation of the original title of 187 words! The complete title made the origin and extent of the 'concert for prayer' explicit. It begins as follows: *'An humble attempt to promote explicit agreement and visible union of God's people in extraordinary prayer for the revival of religion and the advancement of Christ's kingdom on earth, pursuant to the Scripture promises and prophecies concerning the last time.'*

Edwards was well acquainted with the details of the concert for prayer through personal correspondence with ministers in Scotland. Although he does not mention it, it is probable that their idea was partly inspired by himself. In the closing paragraphs of his book, *Some Thoughts Concerning the Present Revival, etc,* published in 1742 and read widely in Scotland, he recommended that ministers might make a draft of a covenant with God; 'Suppose the matter be fully proposed and explained to the people, and, after sufficient opportunity for consideration, they be led ... particularly to subscribe to the covenant. Suppose also all appear together on a day of prayer and fasting, publicly to own it before God in his house.' Here he gives an example of the 1596 General Assembly, which was inspired to dedicate itself to concerted prayer and repentance by the bold and stirring words of a preacher by the name of John Davidson.

In *An Humble Attempt,* Edwards was able to refute contemporary charges that covenanted prayer was a novelty. He cited examples of such schemes in London in 1712 and in Scotland in 1732 and 1735, and argued that those whose proposals he now endorsed were 'no separatists or schismatics, but quiet, peaceable members and ministers of Scotland'. He included in the book a full copy of the 1746 memorial.

A foremost feature in the concert for prayer was the unity experienced by those of different denominations. For instance, while the concert was mobilized by Presbyterians in Scotland, an Anglican reaped one of the richest harvests of souls ever recorded in Cambuslang, Scotland. Then the concept received its clearest and most compelling expression in the treatise written by Jonathan Edwards, a Congregationalist, but eventually, as we shall see, it spread among the Baptists and from them to the Methodists, with an outcome of staggering proportions.

The concert of prayer takes root in England

John Sutcliff (1752-1814), who was Carey's one-time pastor and tutor, was the key figure by whom the Concert for Prayer came down from Scotland. Sutcliff's friend John Ryland Jr (1753-1825) was in correspondence with John Erskine *(1721-1803),* a well-known minister in Scotland who sent *An Humble Attempt* to him. Later he shared it with Sutcliff.

Edwards' treatise challenged Sutcliff to pray for the blessing of the Holy Spirit on the Particular Baptist denomination. The treatise begins with the opening up of Zechariah *8:20-22:* 'This is what the Lord Almighty says: "Many peoples and the inhabitants of many cities will yet come, and the inhabitants of one city will go to another and say, 'Let us go at once to entreat the Lord and seek the Lord Almighty. I myself am going.' And many peoples and powerful nations will come to Jerusalem to seek the Lord Almighty and to entreat him."'

Edwards' appeal for the establishment of regular prayer meetings, where there could be fervent prayer that God 'would appear for the help of his church' , so impressed Sutcliff that at the next meeting of the Baptist churches of the Northamptonshire Association, to which his church at Olney belonged, he proposed that monthly prayer meetings be set up to pray for the outpouring of God's Spirit and the revival of religion. This proposal was adopted by the representatives of the twenty or so churches of the Association and a circular letter was sent to their churches which began by urging them 'to wrestle with God for the effusion of his Holy Spirit'. Practical suggestions as to the way in which to implement these monthly prayer meetings then followed. It was recommended that there be corporate prayer for one hour on the first Monday evening of each month.

'The grand object of [this] prayer is to be that the Holy Spirit may be poured down on our ministers and churches, that sinners may be converted, the saints edified, the interest of religion revived, and the name of God glorified. At the same time, remember, we trust you will not confine your requests to your own societies [i.e. churches]; or to your own immediate connection [i.e. denomination]; let the whole interest of the Redeemer be affectionately remembered, and the spread of the gospel to the most distant parts of the habitable globe be the object of your most fervent requests. We shall rejoice if any other Christian societies of our own or other denominations will unite with us, and do now invite them most cordially to join heart and hand in the attempt.'

The treatise makes an earnest appeal as follows: 'Who can tell what the consequences of such an united effort in prayer may be! Let us plead with God the many gracious promises of his Word, which relate to the future success of his gospel. He has said, "I will yet for this be enquired of by the House of Israel to do it for them, I will increase them with men like a flock." Surely we have love enough for Zion to set apart one hour at a time, twelve times in a year, to seek her welfare' (Ezek. 36:37).

Michael Haykin, writing in *Reformation Today,* comments on this treatise by drawing attention to three points. Firstly, he notes 'the conviction that reversing the downward trend of the Particular Baptists could not be accomplished by mere human zeal, but must be effected by an outpouring of the Spirit of God'.

'Sutcliff later observed: "The outpouring of the divine Spirit ... is the grand promise of the New Testament . . . his influences are the soul, the great animating soul of all religion. These withheld, divine ordinances are empty cisterns, and spiritual graces are withering flowers. These suspended, the greatest human abilities labour in vain, and the noblest efforts fail of success."

'In both this text and that of the circular letter cited above there is evidence of what Richard Lovelace has called "a theology of radical dependence on the Spirit", a recognition that the Spirit is the true agent of renewal and revival.'

Secondly Haykin observes that 'There is the "inclusive" nature of the praying. As the Particular Baptists of the Northamptonshire Association gathered together to pray they were urged not to think simply of their own churches or even denomination, but to embrace in prayer other Baptist churches and other denominations. The Kingdom consists of more than Baptists! In fact, other denominations were encouraged to join them in praying for revival.' Then thirdly he notes, 'There is the distinct missionary emphasis: pray that the gospel be spread 'to the most distant parts of the habitable globe"!⁴

Before we go on to observe a contemporary example of a concert for prayer we should take to heart the amazing answer which the Lord gave to these prayers.

The subsequent great awakening of 1790 to 1840, called the 'Forgotten Revival'

Referring to John Sutcliff's call to prayer, which was an extension of the concert for prayer, Paul Cook maintains that this call to prayer had the effect of concentrating the minds of God's people on the primary needs of the churches, namely, divine visitati

Continuing on this theme, Cook declares, 'I believe that it was this call to prayer which prepared the hearts of God's people in this land and which prevailed with God and brought about the subsequent revivals which so gloriously blessed our nation. They broke out in 1791 and continued for some fifty years until the 1840s. All over the British Isles, God answered the prayers of his people.'

Whereas the first awakening was a pioneering period, that to which we now refer to as 'the Forgotten Revival' was a time when the land was saturated with the gospel. The statistics bear this out.

In 1791, the year when John Wesley died, the Wesleyan Methodists in Britain had 72,000 members and half a million adherents attending their places of worship. After the death of John Wesley there were divisions and secessions from Wesleyan Methodism yet, despite these, by 1828 they had grown from 72,000 to 245,000 and within the next fifteen years another 100,000 members were added, so that by the year 1850 Wesleyan Methodism numbered 360,000 members, a fivefold increase in sixty years

Such an increase was due to more than human activity!

The Primitive Methodists, who began as just a handful in 1807, grew to 50,000 within a period of eighteen years. When their greatest leader, Hugh Bourne, died in 1851, a year when a religious census was taken throughout the nation, they had

110,000 members and some 230,000 adherents. Their numbers were not made up of sheep stolen from Wesleyan Methodism; almost exclusively the Primitive Methodists were built up as a result of the conversion of ordinary working-class people. It was a converting movement and the only explanation for that amazing development was the power of God.

In the same period, the Particular Baptists, who had been bypassed by the previous revival, experienced a marvelous expansion. In 1801 the Particular Baptists had 652 places of worship. By 1851, they had 2,000 chapels and 400,000 adherents. What an amazing expansion within just fifty years! Wales furnishes an interesting example of the revival that took place amongst the Baptists. In 1790 there were just forty-eight Baptist chapels in Wales and almost all of them shamefully established by sheep-stealing from the Independents and the Calvinistic Methodists. But a glorious converting work began towards the end of the eighteenth century so that by 1851, instead of forty-eight chapels they had fifty-six places of worship, a tenfold increase in sixty years.

The Congregationalists or Independents, as they have sometimes been called, in the main opposed the evangelical revival. Apart from notable exceptions, such as Philip Doddridge and one or two others, they opposed the converting work that went on in the days of Whitefield and Wesley and the other great preachers of the eighteenth century. However, they were so powerfully revived in the early nineteenth century that by 1851 they had between a half and three quarters of a million adherents, especially in the new industrial and urban cities of this country, so that many of the urban populations have been evangelized by the Congregationalists.

In viewing these figures we discover that in the fifty years between 1790 and 1840, 1,500,000 people were gathered in England and Wales alone, constituting one out of every ten people in the country, converted and brought into the nonconformist chapels. It was this great work of God which subsequently shaped the nation and indeed helped to establish a middle class, which became the basis of prosperity and laid the foundation of the great reforms of the Victorian age. This second evangelical awakening assumed even greater proportions in America, which can be documented by an abundance of materials in print there.

The character and power of the revival

It assists us greatly when we enter into the nature of a revival and are thus able to understand something of its power. In 1791 the Lord answered the prayers of his people in Wales. One area affected was Bala, under the ministry of the renowned Rev. Thomas Charles.

In a letter dated 9 Dec 1791, Charles described the scene in the town on the evening of the day the revival broke, when 'There was nothing to be heard from one end of town to the other but the cries and groans of people in distress of soul.' The effect of the visitation was that 'The state and welfare of the soul is become the great concern of the country. Scores of the wildest and most inconsiderate of people have been awakened.' Charles quotes cases of deep conviction so strong as almost to drive people mad, though, he tells us, when delivered, these same people had consolation and joy which were correspondingly great.

In another letter written a few weeks later, Charles stated that the revival in Bala was continuing 'with great power and glory'. He says, 'I can hardly believe my eyes sometimes when I see in the chapel those who were the most faithful servants of Satan weeping with a sense of sin and danger and crying out for mercy.'

Two years later, at the beginning of 1794, in a letter written to a correspondent in Scotland, Charles observes that In the course of the last year the almighty power of the gospel has been most gloriously manifested in different parts of our country. Last spring, there was a very great and general awakening through a very large and populous district of Caernarvonshire, in the space of three months some hundreds were brought under concern about their souls.' He had earlier expressed the view that 'Unless we are favoured with frequent revivals and a strong powerful work of the Spirit of God we shall degenerate and have only a name to live. Religion will soon lose its vigour, the ministry will hardly retain its lustre and glory and iniquity will in consequence abound.'

We have been living on the capital of previous revivals and that capital has become very sparse. Thomas Charles believed, as did Jonathan Edwards, and the ministers of that time, that without continuing frequent revivals, supernatural visitations of God, the church inevitably degenerates.

This was also the outlook of the Wesleyan Methodists of England, who were experiencing similar revivals at that time. William Bramwell was one of the most powerful of the Wesleyan preachers during the 1790s and the first two decades of the nineteenth century. He was a man of prayer whose life and ministry are a challenge to any minister of the gospel. This man became God's instrument in a great revival of religion which broke out in Dewsbury in 1792. Believing in the necessity of revival, he had been praying fervently. Such a remarkable assurance was given to him that the revival would be granted that he recorded these words in his journal before the event: 'As I was praying in my room I received an answer from God in a particular way and had the revival discovered to me in its manner and effects. I had no more doubt. All my grief was gone. I could say, "The Lord will come, I know he will come, and come suddenly."' That is what these men meant by prevailing prayer.

Soon afterwards he described how an amazing spirit of prayer was given to the people: 'Several who were the most prejudiced were suddenly struck down and in agonies groaned for deliverance. The work continued in almost every meeting. Our love feasts began to be crowded and people from every neighbouring circuit visited us. Great numbers found pardon.'[5]

It should be noted that there were no altar calls but rather a profound doctrine of personal repentance. There was no such thing as hurrying convicted souls to a decision and to assurance. The preachers relied on the Holy Spirit to do his work without human manipulation.

Examples of concerts of prayer

In 1727 a visitation of the Spirit came to the community of believers at Herrnhut in Moravia. Religious refugees from various parts of Europe had turned Herrnhut into a thriving community, but it was through the spiritual visitation of 1727 that a great missionary passion was born. Doctrinal differences that had caused contention were laid aside and a strong spirit of unity began to prevail. A prayer vigil was begun that continued around the clock, seven days a week, without interruption for more than 100 years. The Moravians sent out more missionaries than all Protestants (and Anglicans) had sent out in the previous 2 centuries.[6]

To leap over the centuries to our present time, I would refer to the extraordinary usefulness and inspiration of the book *Operation World* by Patrick Johnstone.[7] The production of this book and the background to its preparation reveal the interweaving of prayer with practical action.

The story began in 1900 when Dr Andrew Murray, the great man of God in South Africa, wrote a book with the title, *The key to the missionary problem*. In that book, he issued a challenge calling the churches to hold a 'week of prayer for the world'. We have no record of the implementation of that challenge, but it lay in the mind of Hans van Staden, who was the founder of the Dorothea Mission in South Africa. In 1963, Hans van Staden began the mission to take the gospel to the rapidly developing urban slums of Southern Africa.

8. Our present decline compels it

The United Kingdom (fifty-eight million) is part of the European Union which in 2005 consisted of twenty-five nations. The larger of these are Germany (eighty-two million), France (fifty-nine million), Italy (fifty-seven million), Spain (thirty-nine million) and Poland (thirty-eight million). Some of these countries involved are the most poverty-stricken, spiritually speaking, in the world today. Even the rather optimistic statistics cited from *Operation World* show a pitiful proportion of evangelicals: Italy 0.9%, Spain 0.4%, and France 0.8%. Nothing but a heaven-sent spiritual awakening will remove the gross darkness that covers these nations, and only a God-given awakening will prevent Britain from sliding down into similar spiritual poverty.

A megashift in the way people in Western Europe think has taken place since the 1970s from modernism to postmodernism. An integral part of postmodern culture is a-morality, or to be more plain, selective morality. It is still deemed a crime to steal or to commit murder. However the commandment 'Thou shalt not commit adultery', is a part of God's law which is deleted. It is as though that commandment has been scraped out of the tablets of stone on which the ten commandments were written. Whereas in the previous generation premarital sex was regarded as adultery now it is the norm. Whereas marriage was regarded as the norm now it is not. This disregard for the biblical foundation of marriage and God's law which protects it has resulted in desperate damage to society.

A leading article in *The Daily Telegraph* (30 September 2005) begins as follows, 'Marriage is in terminal decline, government figures showed yesterday. Within twenty-five years nearly half of all men in their mid-forties and more than a third of women will not have walked up the aisle.'

Reaping the whirlwind of Postmodernism

The breakdown of family life has had catastrophic results on society. Politicians realise that this subject must be addressed. In the Conservative leadership contest which took place in November 2005 both David Davis and David Cameron placed this subject at the top of their political agendas. Davis declared, 'Families are the foundation stone of society. Tax and benefit systems must help, not hinder, the aim of stable families'. Cameron likewise placed the family at the top of his priorities. He declared that we must respond to the challenge of social breakdown by actively supporting marriage through the tax and benefits system.

Bad doctrine and bad principles will result in bad life. So much has changed since the West moved away from a Christian base which though nominal still served to give a sense of stability and direction. 'It was only one generation ago that the Bible and the Ten Commandments were taught in our schools. There was discipline in the home and in the classroom. The parent supported the teacher. Common decency prevailed in the community. There was respect for authority in the home and in society. The extended family was a protection against crime. Divorce was rare and having a child out of wedlock was looked on as a scandal. Homosexuality was not so much as named among us. The press and the broadcasting authorities conformed to standards of morality and decency.'[1]

The most devastating effects of a Postmodern society and the permissive society of the 1960s that preceded it are the downgrading of marriage and the break up of family life. Now as we see from leading politicians downwards the custom is for couples to live together and perhaps consider marriage at a future time. Allied with that is a massive divorce rate now running at a terrifying fifty percent. The effects of this on children is appalling not to mention the destructive effects on the parents. Infidelity is the main reason leading to divorce. The media have contributed to decline. The programs that promote promiscuity and which border on pornography are destructive. Criticism is scorned by most program managers.

Peter Hitchins traces out the changing attitude that has taken place. 'Shame and stigma, which once both defended respectable marriage and heaped misery on the poor bastard and his wretched mother, have disappeared. Instead, there is the slower, vaguer more indirect misery of a society where fewer and fewer children have two parents, and where more and more women are married to the State.'[2] 'In the post-war years the number of births outside marriage actually dropped for thirteen years between 1945 and 1959. In 1959, the Legitimacy Act allowed post facto legitimacy to children whose parents had 'not been free' to marry at the time of their birth. These were humane changes ensuring that the sins of the parents could not be visited on the children. But they also made it easier for the parents to commit those sins without so much fear of the consequences, and they assumed that the old forces of shame and disgrace were purely negative, nasty cobwebs in the corner of an unreformed society which could have no possible purpose in the modern world.'[3] Major changes began in 1987 when a new abridged birth certificate allowed children to conceal their parents' unmarried status.

The demotion of the sacred institution of marriage and the family is seen in the increasing demand for the acceptance of different sexual lifestyles. The Civil Partnership Act took effect from December 2005 in which same sex couples have the same exemptions from Inheritance Tax as husbands and wives. Everyone has equal rights in this area. The recent decision of Parliament to allow homosexual and cohabiting couples to adopt children is an indication of how far some are pushing the equal rights agenda.

A-morality in society brings about a whole raft of painful results. There is the increase of teenage pregnancies, the increase of a variety of sexually transmitted diseases, permanent injury in the realm of trust and relationships. A further hurtful and damaging outcome is what is termed 'Dad's empty chair'. James Wilson of the USA media comments on Dad's empty chair like this: 'boys in father-absent families were twice as likely as those in two-parent ones to go to jail and girls in father-absent families were twice as likely as those in married families to have an out-of-wedlock birth. What all of this means for the rest of society is evident on the evening news programs. Boys without married fathers populate our street gangs, and these gangs are responsible for an inordinately high level of violence. We rely on the police to control gangs, but the important, and often absent, control is that exercised by fathers. A boy growing up without a father has no personal conception of what it means to acquire skills, find a job, support a family, and be loyal to one's wife and children. Research on the link between unemployment rates and crime has shown that the connection is very weak. The connection between crime and father absence is much higher. Boys in single-parent families are also more likely to be idle rather than in school or unemployed and to drop out of high school. These differences are as great for white families as for black and Hispanic ones and as large for advantaged children as for disadvantaged ones.'

Trouble has spilled out into schools in the UK. An area of enormous stress is the breakdown of respect in the classroom as John J. Murray describes it, 'As happened with Rome before its fall, society is taking on coarseness. There is violence in the classroom. Teachers are leaving the profession due to stress. One teacher spoke about advice given to him: "We are being urged to give the kids Mars bars when they are walking around with iron bars." Teenagers engage in loutish behaviour. City streets are less safe, especially at nights. Some of our inner cities have been turned into no-go areas for the police. A chief constable said: "If a couple of parents cannot control their children, how can two of my men control 200?"'

The apostle Paul said that godliness is the basis of righteousness, and unrighteousness flows out of ungodliness (Rom 1:18). What will be the outcome of the increase in alcoholism, drug addiction, violence and crime which evidences the spiritual bankruptcy of Postmodern Western society? Will the generation who have come from broken homes turn to the gospel, or will they continue to seek solace in the very sins which brought their parents and themselves into bondage and distress? Will they find new life in Christ, or be lured into the increasing array of cults or the occult?'

Retired clergyman Dennis Peterson writes, 'The effect of disrupted families is disruptive child behaviour. One of the main reasons for teachers leaving the profession is despair at pupil behaviour. I met a young lad who had about a hundred scars on his back where he had been stabbed by things like compass points. A teacher recently burst into tears as she told me of the fear she has from violence in her school.'[5] During October 2005 newspapers published photos of a girl whose face had been slashed by knives by fellow girl pupils. That could be an isolated exceptional event but it is not. The increase of violence in schools is a national problem.

If the decline in morals and behaviour has taken place as described then surely this will reflect in the levels of crime recorded in England and Wales. This is a controversial field because of the possibility of manipulating statistics to prove a point. However there are basic trends which are inescapable. The level of crime increased fifty-fold from 1921 when 103,258 crimes were recorded to 5.2 million recorded cases of crime in 2001. Another statistic concerns the prison population. The prison population for England and Wales increased dramatically to 77,000 in 2005, a rise of seventy percent since 1993 when it was 44,500. In March 2005 eighty-two of the 139 prisons in England and Wales were overcrowded.[6]

Decline of the churches

From the moral decline in Great Britain we now turn to the state of the churches. The steep decline in church membership which is well illustrated in the graphs can be traced back to the rise of liberalism during the nineteenth century and the rejection of the Bible as a reliable book. Gradually moralistic teaching replaced the gospel of salvation from eternal damnation and wherever this has taken place certain demise has followed. Great Britain is increasingly a land of church buildings where once the gospel was preached but now those buildings have been turned into flats, offices or warehouses.

An apt commentary on Great Britain is found in Judges 2:10, 'After that whole generation had been gathered to their fathers, another generation grew up, who knew neither the LORD nor what he had done for Israel.'

An examination of the graphs will show that the once thriving Methodist denomination is spiralling down to extinction. The
same is true of the United Reformed Church.

The situation in the Church of England illustrates the point
made above that the crucial issue is gospel preaching. There are
thriving evangelical Anglican churches but there are not enough
to withstand the overall decline. Up and down England there are
more and more Anglican churches which are closing. Soon we
are told fifty percent of the Anglican clergy will be women. That
sends out a two-fold message. First the Scripture teaching about
male leadership is unheeded and that usually means that a liberal
view of Scripture prevails. Secondly it sends out a message that
the Church is now so weak that there are insufficient men to lead.
That confirms a state of serious decline and time and time again
that decline proves to be terminal.

Similar to the Anglican Church is the Baptist Union denomination. The Baptist Union consists of a mixture of liberal and
evangelical pastors and women pastors. Unless held together by
strong social ties the liberal churches will decline since there is no
gospel to draw sinners to be saved. The evangelical churches vary
in quality but the Baptist Union as a whole is in decline as the
graph shows.

Where evangelicalism in a nation is thriving it is hard for the
cults to grow because the light of the gospel shines brightly so that
denial of the deity of Jesus is hard to promote. The graphs show
the rapid growth of Jehovah's Witnesses and Mormons.

The Pentecostal denominations show a gradual growth. The
Grace Baptists and their next of kin the Reformed Baptists form a
small part of evangelicalism. The Reformed Baptists are less traditional in style and many of their churches show healthy growth.
Many small Grace churches are ageing and are unlikely to survive.
There are exceptions. Where a new pastor takes over in a church
and evangelizes energetically the recovery is often remarkable.

Commentary on the graphs

The graphs show membership of churches and other religious
groups for the twentieth century and a prediction for the next fifty

years. These graphs are not meant to be exhaustive as regards religious groups but provide a snapshot of the main trends occurring in Great Britain.

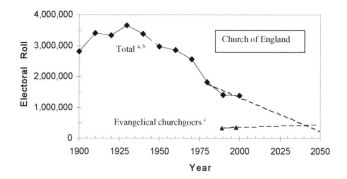

The Church of England. In an article in *The Churchman* (Summer 2005) retired clergyman Dennis Peterson laments the fact that we have lost sight of the 1859-60 revival in England in which the membership of the Church of England grew phenomenally from eighteen percent of the population to twenty-seven percent. This fact in itself reminds us that only an outpouring of the Holy Spirit can bring about a radical change. It is the preaching of the gospel alone that makes the difference. There is no hope for denominations which have been taken over by liberals who deny the principal doctrines of the Bible. It is the presence of vibrant evangelical churches within the Anglican body that moderates the decline. The nominal part of the Church of England is fading away at such a pace that eventually only the evangelical constituency will be left to function in any realistic way. There is a major crisis in the Anglican communion because funding is running out to maintain the fabric of empty churches all over the land.

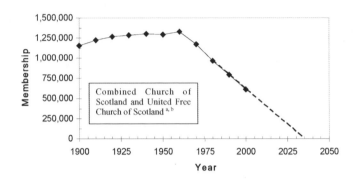

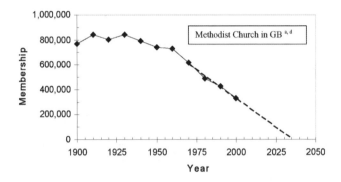

Church of Scotland. About thirty years ago a story was spread that all the evangelical ministers in the Church of Scotland combined would be able to fit into a telephone box. Yet through the ministry of several leaders such as William Still the proportion of evangelical ministers increased to about forty percent. That might be over optimistic. Today it may be much less. The decline certainly is very evident from the graph.

The Methodists. The decline of Methodism is dramatic. Since the saving gospel of Christ has been abandoned it is visibly evident that the Holy Spirit has abandoned this denomination. Methodist church buildings all over the land have been sold to be turned into other purposes.

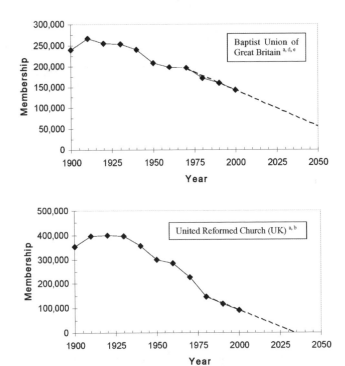

The Baptist Union. Since the Downgrade Controversy of 1887 –1892 in which C. H. Spurgeon was the leader of the evangelical Baptists there has been no change in the BU. The BU leaders have not come to grips with the need of reformation. That is impossible because liberals occupy the seats of influence and power. For instance when Michael Taylor used the platform of the annual BU assembly in 1971 to deny the deity of Christ no discipline was exercised. At least twenty churches seceded from the Union. What security is there for future generations when there is no guarantee of doctrinal fidelity? Baptist Unions vary from country to country. In South Africa the battle with the unbelieving liberals was won in the 1920s. Fidelity to the Word of God has followed ever since.

The United Reformed Church. This body too has been invaded by modernist theology. It is only a matter of time before this denomination becomes extinct.

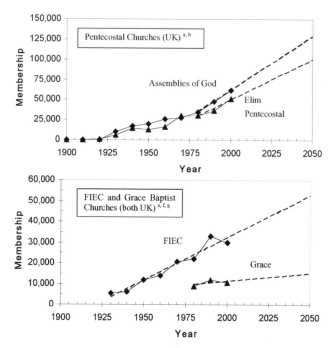

The Pentecostal denominations. The graphs of the two largest Pentecostal Churches show growth. We are reminded by this that when the gospel is preached with zeal and where there is concerted evangelism there will be growth. There are many other, smaller, charismatic groupings not shown which also show growth.

FIEC (Fellowship of Independent Evangelical Churches), Grace Baptist and Reformed Baptist churches. The graphs for the FIEC show an encouraging upward trend. The manner in which unity among evangelical churches has spread is heartening. According to Psalm 133 where there is unity in the truth there the Lord bestows his blessing. Closely allied to the FIEC are Grace Baptists and Reformed Baptists. Contemporaneity is a major issue in these churches. Where leaders cling to Scripture and at the same time encourage young people there is growth whereas where strict tradition for tradition's sake is maintained there sterility prevails. The saying is true that a reformed church always needs to reform testing everything in the light of Scripture.

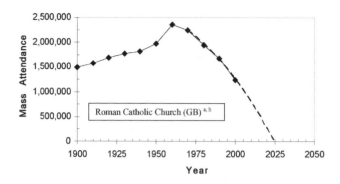

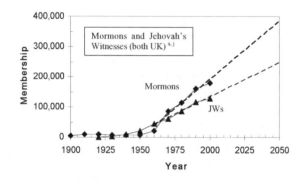

Roman Catholicism. The decline of Roman Catholicism is widespread in Western Europe especially in France and Great Britain. The Roman Catholic Church has served to keep families cemented. Spain is an example. But Catholic influence is waning in Spain too. Spain, once a bastion of Catholic culture and commitment, has now embraced same-sex marriage. Spain became the third country to legalize gay marriage.

Mormons and JWs. When the light of the gospel shines brightly it is difficult for cults to grow. When there is biblical illiteracy such as prevails in the UK today there the cults have a free hand.

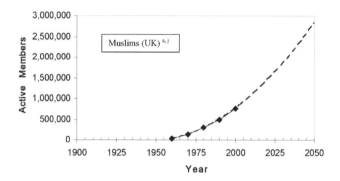

Islam. The increase of Muslims is mostly by large families and by immigration. What possibility is there of revival in such an age of decadence as our own? We must not forget the situation that preceded the eighteenth-century Awakening. We have liberalism; they had deism. We have the drug menace; they had rum. We have abortion; they had the degradation of the slave trade. We have contempt for the gospel, especially in places of influence; so did they. We have bishops who tolerate practising homosexuals in the ministry and the blatant public denial of the deity of Christ by one of their number; eighteenth-century Britain also suffered a lethargic clergy. Yet in spite of all the obstacles the Holy Spirit intervened in a marvelous way, using humble prayers and a handful of godly leaders.

If ever we should seek to unite in prayer for revival it is now! The social decadence of our Western world demands it.

Footnotes to graphs

A. Graphs drawn using data obtained from 'UK Christian Handbook Religious Trends No.2 2000/01' Ed Dr Peter Brierley Published 1999 by Christian Research, London, ISBN 1853211346, and 'UK Christian Handbook Religious Trends No. 4 2003/2004' Ed Dr Peter Brierley Published 2003 by Christian Research, London, ISBN 1853211494. Figures for Northern Ireland are generally excluded as it is relatively small and not typical of the rest of the UK.

B. Prediction is obtained by drawing a linear best fit line through the values for the years 1980 – 2000

C. Values for evangelical churchgoers were calculated using data from 'Coming Up Trumps' by Peter Brierley. Published 2004 by Authentic Media, Milton Keynes ISBN 1850785481. Prediction is obtained by drawing a linear best fit line through the values for the years 1989 – 1998

D. Prediction is obtained by drawing a linear best fit line through the values for the years 1970 – 2000

E. Additional information obtained from Baptist Union, Didcot, UK

F. Prediction for FIEC is obtained by drawing a linear best fit line through the values for the years 1930 – 2000

G. Prediction for Grace Baptist Churches is obtained by drawing a linear best fit line through the values for the years 1980 – 2000

H. Prediction is obtained by drawing a curve (second order poly-nominal) through the values for the years 1970 – 2000.

Warm gratitude is expressed to Dr Stephen Collins for his work on the graphs and to Dr Peter Brierley for his advice on the graphs.

9. The promises of Scripture urge it

In his *Humble attempt to promote explicit and visible union of God's people in extraordinary prayer for revival* Edwards refers to a number of prophecies and observes that 'There has been nothing yet brought to pass, in any measure, to answer these prophecies.[1]

In another work he comments, 'The prophecies of Scripture give us reason to think that God has things to accomplish, which have never yet been seen.[2]

Do the Scriptures promise great revivals in this dispensation? That is a very important question. Do those Scriptures promise that the gospel will be victorious over all opposition? That question too is vital. If we believe that the descriptions apply to the extension of the Messiah's kingdom then we should feel constrained to explore their meaning. All Scripture has a moral application. As we view the prophecies they create hope and vision which in turn lead to intercession. A bright future prospect for Christ's kingdom on earth inspires missionary zeal and enterprise. When the way is hard and exacting, the ultimate victory envisaged will engender courage and impart perseverance.

The full title used by Jonathan Edwards for his treatise calling for a concert of prayer specifies that 'The attainment of visible union and explicit agreement of God's people through the world, in extraordinary prayer for revival, is pursuant to the Scripture promises and prophecies concerning the last time.' He refers to several scriptures in this connection, such as Micah 4 and Isaiah 60:2-4.

The promotion of prayer was obviously the main thrust of his treatise, which explains why he begins with an exposition of

Zechariah 8:20-22. The text reads: 'This is what the Lord Almighty says: "Many peoples and the inhabitants of many cities will ye come, and the inhabitants of one city will go to another and say, 'Let us go at once to entreat the Lord and seek the Lord Almighty. I myself am going.' And many peoples and powerful nations will come to Jerusalem to seek the Lord Almighty and to entreat him."' Edwards asserts of this passage: 'There never happened anything, from the time of the prophet Zechariah to the time of Christ to answer this prophecy.'

From an examination of Edwards' exposition it is clear that he is not being presumptuous about the text, as though the fact that it sounds good is sufficient basis to encourage prayer. No! Having scrutinized the meaning and context and the actual words of the Hebrew text, he makes five practical observations and applies each in turn, a synopsis of which runs as follows.

1. The duty of prayer

Prayer is repeatedly emphasized in Zechariah 8:20-22. The prayer described is extraordinary. It is with the specific purpose of intercession, of seeking the fulfilment of great good, that strong nations unite in their mission of prayer.

2. The good that shall be sought by prayer, which is God himself

The expression 'seeking the Lord' is often used in the Scriptures and it implies that God himself is the great good to be desired and sought after. It is the characteristic of the saints that they seek God.

> O God, you are my God,
>   earnestly I seek you;
> my soul thirsts for you
>   (Ps. 63:1).

If the Lord has been absent from the church for a long time then we must seek his return.

3. We must observe the unity of those who are many people and strong nations

Multitudes in different parts of the world will unite and conspire in this matter of seeking the Lord. In this manner religion shall be propagated until the awakening reaches those who are in the highest stations, and till whole nations be awakened, and there be at length an accession of many of the chief nations of the world to the church of God.'

At this point Edwards suggests that the accessions to the church will be vast and he cites the next verse, namely Zechariah *8:23:* 'This is what the Lord Almighty says: "In those days ten men from all languages and nations will take firm hold of one Jew by the hem of his robe and say, 'Let us go with you, because we have heard that God is with you.' "' Obviously we would take the term 'Jew' in the sense expressed by Paul in Romans *2:28-29,* that is in the spiritual, or regenerate sense. Zechariah in making his prophecy could hardly use the word 'Christian'. In an awakening it is Christians that are sought out to give knowledge, counsel, comfort and assurance.

4. The agreement of many peoples and strong nations is explicit

In other words, there is clarity about the objectives sought. The peoples and nations understand the promises which form the basis of their prayers. They are united and resolute in their purpose to go together at a set time. There is no apathy or sluggishness here.

5. The manner of prayer agreed on is urgent

'Let us go at once to pray' or as the NKJV expresses it, 'Let us continue to go.' Edwards observes that the text literally means, 'Let us go in going.' In contemporary language, 'Let's go for it.' The Hebrew expression involves what he calls an ingemination, which is a word we do not use today. To geminate means to repeat or to arrange in pairs. A similar form of language is that used to Abraham: 'In multiplying, I will multiply,' meaning multiply exceedingly. In the text in question the idea is that there is strength and quality in the going. There is a determination in this going to seek the Lord together. There is the element in which the answer, 'No!' will not be acceptable, as Jacob insisted, 'I will not let you go unless you bless me!' Vast blessings are promised. They are to be obtained through asking (Isa. 62:6,7).

What are the promises to be laid hold of?

If we are to engage in a concert of prayer together then we need to be sure of the promises and prophecies to be laid hold of. It is futile to plead for the fulfilment of something that is not really promised. The question comes to mind whether the prophetic passages from the Psalms, Isaiah, Ezekiel and other prophets, used by Edwards to support his exposition from Zechariah, might be taken out of context. Have they not already found fulfilment in the return of the Jews from Babylon? Furthermore are not the passages cited from Zechariah, Ezekiel and Isaiah of the poetic kind in which hyperbole abounds? Isn't it misguided to take literally that which might have been intended as beautiful language?

Is it possible that Edwards and those of his kind were carried away by wishful thinking? We would love to see the triumph of the gospel and therefore may fall into the trap of wishful thinking. To support our ideas we may then twist or exaggerate language which was never intended to be taken literally.

These questions demand serious treatment and call for a substantial answer. It is true that Edwards and many others of his school do not attempt to classify the passages they quote, but seem to take it for granted that they refer to these last times, namely the messianic age. The Puritans believed in the advance of Christ's kingdom until a time of universal conquest. They referred to that time as 'the latter day glory'. An example of this approach is seen in the writing of John G. Lorimer, *Encouragements from the promises and prophecies of Scripture*.[3] Lorimer declares, 'The Word of God teems with intimations, direct or indirect — with statements or inferences — with assurances and prophecies of a day of coming universal revival.' He believed in a latter time when there would be the glory of knowledge, holiness, unity and joy.

Also as a representative of that belief in a latter-day glory he believed that 'The almost insuperable obstacles to the progress of the gospel will be suddenly destroyed,' not gradually but, 'To make his own arm the more visible, and draw the attention of men more impressively, he strikes down the enemy when even his people are not looking for the blow.'[4]

A classification of the promises and prophecies is important because a collation and comparison of the texts helps to determine how far we should go in understanding the meaning conveyed. I suggest four categories, which we shall examine in the following paragraphs.

1. The sufferings and glories of the Messiah as portrayed by Isaiah

The principles concerned with the kingship of Christ are similar in Isaiah 2:1-4; 9:1-7; 11 and Isaiah 65:17-25 and are the same as we find in the Psalms. We will come to these presently, but let us look first at the passages in Isaiah which describe the Servant of Jahweh, his sufferings and the glories that will follow.

Isaiah 42 describes this Servant as meek and unassuming yet successful, for he will establish justice on the earth. His law will go far and wide because the islands will put their hope in him. Isaiah 49:1-7 complains that the work of the Servant seems to be of no purpose and his strength has been spent in vain. Jahweh's response to that is that his Servant will not only restore the tribes of Jacob but he will be made a light for the Gentiles and be their salvation to the ends of the earth. This salvation will not be an insignificant thing hidden in a corner for,

> Kings will see you and rise up,
> princes will see and bow down,
> because of the Lord, who is faithful.

Isaiah 50:6-9 and 52:13-53:12 describe in more detail the agonies endured by the Servant on whom the Lord lays our iniquities. The outcome will be far-reaching, for 'he will sprinkle many nations'. He will see the result of the suffering of his soul and be satisfied. Commensurate with the Messiah's sufferings, which are without equal, is the reward given to him in all the earth. His sufferings are without equal because of his unique nature, combined with the unique nature of his shame, for he was 'stricken by God, smitten by him, and afflicted'. So his glory will be without equal. Several passages which follow in Isaiah are redolent with descriptions of that glory as seen in the advance and universal sway of his kingdom.

Following the description of his sufferings, the extent of the future glory of Zion is described in Isaiah 54. Zion will have a numerous offspring. Leupold translates 54:3: 'For you will burst forth in every direction, and your descendants will take possession of the Gentiles; and they shall cause desolate cities to be populated.' The substance of Isaiah 55 is that the free invitations of the gospel are to be universally made.

Observing the principle of Romans 11:17-24, namely, that Gentiles have been grafted into the olive tree and are supported by the root, we continue with the theme of Zion's future glory as portrayed by Isaiah from chapter 59:20 onwards. This text is quoted in Romans 11:26. The promise is that the Lord will carry forward his work 'like a pent-up flood that the breath of the Lord drives along'. The Redeemer will come to Zion, for he has a covenant with his people to take away their sins. Paul applies this passage to the Messiah and to the repentance of ethnic Israel (Rom. 11:26-27). Thereafter, the glory of the Lord shines on the nations which have been in gross darkness.

> See, darkness covers the earth
>   and thick darkness is over the peoples,
> but the Lord rises upon you
>   and his glory appears over to you.
> Nations will come to your light,
>   and kings to the brightness of your dawn
>   (Isa. 60:1-3).

The riches of the Gentile nations are willingly brought to serve the interests of the Messiah.

The wealth on the seas will be brought to you,
  to you the riches of the nations will come

(Isa. 60:5).

Your gates will always stand open,
  they will never be shut, day or night,
  so that men may bring you the wealth of the nations
— their kings led in triumphal procession.
For the nation or kingdom that will not serve you will perish;
  it will be utterly ruined

(Isa. 60:11-12).

The picture is filled with the glory of God in the display of his grace and favour which is multiplied on a scale which we now find incredible:

The least of you will become a thousand,
  the smallest a mighty nation.
I am the Lord;
  in its time I will do this swiftly

(Isa. 60:22).

Similar in character to the passage quoted above is Haggai 2:7-8: 'I will shake all nations, and the desired of all nations will come, and I will fill this house with glory.' The Hebrew verb for 'will come' is plural and requires a plural subject, so this verse means 'The treasures [desirable things] of all nations shall come in.' The context, as in Isaiah 60, speaks of riches of the nations. 'The silver is mine and the gold is mine' (Hag. 2:8). The principle has been universally observed that when revival comes to the Lord's people, then there is no shortage of funds to provide for all the needs. These may be for missionary endeavour, seminaries, Bible translation and publication, literature work, old people's homes, orphanages, or funds for building complexes adequate to accommodate his work. When hearts are opened purses open too! When hearts are cool the funds are stinted.

In his exposition of Isaiah 9:1-7, Leupold refers to the child who has four names. He is Wonderful Counsellor, Mighty God, the Father of Eternity, the Prince of Peace. As King he will take the throne of his father David and rule in a kingdom which grows and increases to enormous proportions. The nature of this rule and its increase is described as something which first becomes established as supreme and then prevails by way of teaching and understanding (Isa. 2:1-4). The teaching will eventually take hold upon the nations so that they will train for war no more. The application of this teaching is to the warlike. In other words, it takes place in the arena of this world.

This theme is elaborated further in Isaiah 11. The king has a very humble origin (11:1). He is anointed with the Spirit and is given the spiritual equipment requisite for his ministry (11:2). The character of his rule as one of justice is described (11:3-5). The mighty transformation which this king achieves throughout the earth is portrayed (11:6-9). The revolutionary and powerful manner in which he will effect his purposes is presented (11:10-16).

The principles employed by this king to accomplish his purposes will increasingly prevail until the final transposition comes to the new heavens and new earth. Then the same principles of righteousness and peace will prevail perfectly and universally (Isa. 65:17-25).

These prophecies concern the suffering of the Messiah and the glories that follow. These glories seen in the advance of his kingdom cannot simply be transposed to refer to the final state in the new earth because, with the exception of the last-named prophecy, resistance and conflict are involved. That is not applicable to the eternal state of glory. For instance, an examination of Isaiah 1 1 reveals descriptions of advance, teaching, judgement of the wicked, nations being turned and highways being established for the truth to run along.

2. The kingship of Christ and the extent of his dominion as described in the Psalms

Psalm 110:1 is quoted more in the New Testament than any other text from the psalms:

> The Lord says to my Lord:
> 'Sit at my right hand
> until I make your enemies
> a footstool for your feet.'

The exaltation of Christ is seen in his resurrection, ascension, coronation and coming again to judge the world in righteousness. It is his coronation that is referred to in Psalm 110. The twin roles of King and Priest are united and confirmed in that coronation. The Kingly Priest will employ his authority and power to defeat all his enemies and when that is accomplished he will come and vanquish death, which is the greatest enemy of all (1 Cor. 15:25).

If we take this exaltation of Christ in his kingly office we can trace out, in broad terms, the extent of his dominion in the extension of his kingdom after his ascension. Opposition to the gospel must be viewed in this light. Hence the answer of Jahweh to the rebellious kings, who have rejected and mocked his Anointed One, is to have them in derision. His answer to their folly is that he has set up his own king:

'I have installed my king on Zion, my holy hill' (Ps. 2:6). This king will rule the nations with an iron sceptre: he will dash them to pieces like pottery.

It is vital that we grasp the nature of Christ's rule in its two spheres, *regnum potentiae* and *regnum gratiae,* that is his reign of power by way of administration over the nations, and his reign of grace in the hearts of his people everywhere.

With regard to his reign of power, we witnessed at the end of the 1980s one of the greatest displays of Christ's rule ever seen in this world, namely, the swift breaking and shattering like pottery of the Communist totalitarian hold over Eastern Europe. That which defied all the powers of earth by way of an iron grip, he levelled to dust in a few weeks. The Berlin wall, which we thought impregnable, he broke in pieces overnight. He raises up empires and brings them down again. We see that in the ancient kingdoms of Media, Persia, Greece and Rome. In the modern world, whether nationalist, religious or political, whether capitalist or Communist, whether Islamic or Hindu, no system and no empire will last a moment

longer than he decrees. Let us get this firmly into our minds: our
Lord Messiah reigns!

But that kingdom which will prevail over every other kingdom
and last for ever is the gentle kingdom of his grace in the hearts of
all who are joined to him by faith. Hence the invitation of Psalm
2:8:

> Ask of me,
>> and I will make the nations your inheritance,
>> the ends of the earth your possession.

The reign of power over the governments of this world, their
rise and fall, has a close connection with the reign of grace and the
advance of the gospel. Our King opens doors to countries hitherto
closed, which no man can close.

Always in view is the cross as the only way of atonement and
forgiveness of sins. Psalm 22 gives a vivid description of the sufferings of the Messiah, followed by the dominion that is given to
him:

> All the ends of the earth
>> will remember and turn to the Lord,
> and all the families of the nations
>> will bow before him,
> or dominion belongs to the Lord,
>> and he rules over the nations
>
>   (Ps. 22:27).

The description of the reign of King Messiah is carried forward
in Psalm 72:

> All nations will be blessed through him,
>> and they will call him blessed,

and the psalm concludes with prayer:

> May the whole earth be filled with his glory.
>> Amen and Amen!

3. The promises of God made against dark backgrounds

There could hardly be a gloomier scene than that after the fall of Adam. Yet the promise is made that the seed of the woman would crush the serpent's head (Gen. 3:15). The fulfilment came in the victory of the cross, which is described as the binding of the strong man. Revelation 20:1-3 is the only passage of Scripture which uses the term 'millennium'. Most expositors take the 1,000 years as a symbol of the whole period of this last time, during which all who are united with Christ by faith live and reign with him. Since the other numbers in the Apocalypse are symbolical there is every reason to take the 1,000 years as meaning a full period of time. Whatever we make of the passage, we must consider seriously the binding of Satan in such a way that he is no longer able to deceive the nations. If the nations are not deceived, then surely they are exposed to the glorious light of the gospel. In this way Satan is thwarted. The victory is not his. Even though the whole world is under the control of the evil one (1 John 5:19), he will eventually be crushed, not only with regard to the liberation of individual souls, but also in the curtailing of his rule over the whole world.

Before the birth of Isaac, it seemed to Abraham and Sarah as though the possibility of offspring was nil. That Abraham actually despaired of the promise being fulfilled is seen in his taking Hagar as a wife in order to have a son. Yet the promise was firm and in due time it was fulfilled. Part of the promise was that all nations on earth would be blessed through him (Gen. 12:3; 18:18).

Further scriptures that fall into this category of promises being made against dark backgrounds are Numbers 14:21; Habbakuk 2:14; Daniel 2:35, 44; 7:13-14; Zechariah 9:9-10.

When Moses was discouraged by the rebellion of the children of Israel he was told of God's purpose to fill the earth with his glory (Num. 14:21). Likewise when Habakkuk was deeply depressed and flabbergasted at the destruction of God's city Zion by the Chaldeans, he was assured that 'The revelation awaits an appointed time.' The righteous must live by faith. 'For the earth will be filled with the knowledge of the glory of the Lord, as the waters cover the sea' (Hab. 2:3,4,14).

As a captive in Babylon, Daniel was given the ability to interpret Nebuchadnezzar's dream. The colossal image representing
four great empires, 'an enormous, dazzling statue', was struck by
a rock on its iron and clay feet. The statue tottered and fell. All
vestiges of the empires that it represented have been blown away
by the winds of time, but the rock that struck the statue is a living
rock. Its grows, and goes on growing to become a huge mountain
which fills the whole earth. That rock cut out of a mountain, but
not by human hands, 'will crush all those kingdoms and bring
them to an end, but it will itself endure for ever' (Dan. 2:35, 44).
Zechariah was called to encourage the leaders, Joshua and
Zerubbabel and the people, in their struggle to re-establish the
Commonwealth of Israel. It was a daunting task to accomplish
from dust and rubble. From that time of arduous reconstruction
came messianic promises, including the picture of the Messiah
riding into Jerusalem on the foal of a donkey. The extent of his
dominion is described:

> He will proclaim peace to the nations.
> His rule will extend from sea to sea
>   and from the River to the ends of the earth
>
> (Zech 9:10).

4. Romans 11 and the theory of three epochs

Romans 11 is the key New Testament passage with regard to the
structure of God's purpose during this last time before the return
of Christ. Maurice Roberts expounds this passage in the *Banner
of Truth* magazine.[5] He suggests, 'We may be compelled to break
the mould of our conception of the dealings of God with mankind. We all tend habitually to fall into a twofold conception of the
world's history: Old Testament and New Testament. This is natural
enough because that is the form in which God has given his Word
to us. But it appears from Paul's manner of arguing in Romans
1 1 that God in fact is purposing to bless the world by what may
be termed a threefold progression: first Jews, then Gentiles, then
both together. Not until the Spirit is poured out on Israel in the

future will the high-water mark of God's purposes be reached in his gracious dealings with fallen mankind.'

It is not my purpose to expound Romans 11 here. That has been done by the major commentaries and in a number of books.[6] Interpretations of Romans 11 fall into two principal schools. We will look at the minority grouping first. This school understands that when Paul comes to the conclusion in verse 26, 'And so all Israel will be saved,' he means that all the elect will be saved, or at least the accumulative total of elect Jews over the whole epoch of these last times.[7]

The majority of those who expound Romans 11 in detail, however, maintain that the way in which Paul builds up his contrast between ethnic Israel and the Gentiles is compelling and irresistible. The conclusion they come to is that there is a progression: the Jews, then the Gentiles, and finally a fulness of both Jews and Gentiles.[8] It is argued that the mystery of Israel, 'I do not want you to be ignorant of this mystery, brothers,' is meaningless if it is only that God will save all elect Jews. On at least twenty-three of the twenty-six times that the word 'mystery' is used in the New Testament, it means something that was hidden before but is now made known. That all the elect will be saved was never disputed in the Old Testament. The ingathering of the Gentiles and their relationship to the olive tree, that is Israel, is the very height of mystery according to Ephesians 3:3,6. We read furthermore that God's ways are unsearchable (Rom. 11:33). If a whole chapter is simply asserting that God will save his elect, what is mysterious about that? You could say it in one sentence! Why spend a chapter on it?

Frederic Godet (1812-1900), the Swiss theologian, wrote commentaries of great quality on Luke, John, 1 Corinthians and Romans. On Romans 1 1 he reminds us that the theme from first to last embraces world history: 'According to the whole context, the apostle has in view an epoch in the history of the kingdom of od on this earth, for the subject comprehends the two portions of mankind which Paul has been contrasting with one another throughout the whole chapter. The domain of disobedience, within which God has successively shut them up, leaves both in the end only one issue, that of humbly accepting salvation from the hand of mercy. As Neilsen again says: "Divine impartiality, after having been temporarily veiled by two opposite particularisms, shines forth in the final universalism which embraces in a common salvation all those whom these great judgments have successively humbled and abased."

'Paul teaches only one thing here: that at the close of the history of mankind on this earth there will be an economy of grace in which salvation will be extended to the totality of the nations living here below, and that this magnificent result will be the effect of the humiliating dispensations through which the two halves of mankind shall have successively passed. The apostle had begun this vast exposition of salvation with the fact of universal condemnation; he closes it with that of universal mercy. What could remain to him thereafter but to strike the hymn of adoration and praise? This is what he does in verses 33-36.'[9]

Romans 11 needs to be compared with other New Testament statements such as 2 Corinthians 3:16; Acts 1:6-7; 3:19-20; Luke 13:35; 21:24.

Maurice Roberts concludes his article on 'The Mystery Concerning Israel' by urging the practical relevance of this for the church today: 'Romans 11:25 should have the further effect upon us all of stirring us to pray earnestly and frequently for this great event to come to pass. However blind the Jewish world is today — and blind, alas, it certainly is towards Christ's gospel — we are divinely assured that it will not always be so. No greater encouragement could possibly exist for Jewish missionary enterprise than this. But the same is true for all missionary enterprise and, indeed, for all faithful Christian endeavour of every kind. Israel shall one day come back to God and that event will be as "life from the dead" (v.15) to all the world. This mystery concerning Israel we cannot afford to ignore.'[10]

10. Present day revivals inspire it

Today we can view the countries of the world on a scale unimagined by previous generations. For most of the period of church history it has taken months for news to travel. In a short time an extraordinary revolution in communications has taken place. Now we have instant information by the Internet, e-mail and texting. If a revival broke out in Tokyo, Brisbane, Vancouver, or even in any small town, we could have a full description in seconds just as soon as someone could type the narrative.

If there is tremendous inspiration and spiritual power in hearing or reading about present-day awakenings, how much more in experiencing a revival firsthand! For instance, we notice the connection between the revival in Wales in 1904 and the revival in Latvia in 1934, as seen in the following facts gleaned from *Five Minutes to Midnight,* by T. Omri Jenkins. Thomas Spurgeon, son of C. H. Spurgeon, said of William Fetler of Latvia, 'If my father's seminary had done nothing else than to produce dear Pastor William, it was still worthy of its existence.' William Fetler had visited Wales during the 1904/5 revival, had met Evan Roberts and seen for himself the great evidence of the power of the Spirit in the Principality. He was never the same afterwards. His great burden was that God would send revival to Latvia and Russia. He stirred up his people to pray. Their prayers were heard.

In 1934, James Stewart, a young Scot aged twenty-four, arrived in Riga, capital of Latvia, without an invitation and without warning. He was invited to speak and the power of the Holy Spirit was evidently with him. Meetings were begun which were to continue for five months. Over 2,000 people attended every day. Stewart declared later that it was not only the size of the gathered crowds that was surprising: 'It was the awful sense of the majesty and holiness of God: it was the liberty of the Spirit.' The meetings sometimes went on round the clock with as many people present in the morning as in the afternoon! 'Nobody knew how long a service would last; nobody bothered about the clock; nobody wanted to leave.'[1]

The Twentieth century saw some of the most extensive spiritual awakenings in the history of the church. The most extensive of these has been in China which with 1.3 billion has the largest population in the world. An extended article (30 July 2005) describing the amazing growth of Christianity in China appeared in *The Daily Telegraph*. It comments on the heavy-handed Politburo response to Christianity spreading through town and country and Chinese communities abroad. State-sanctioned churches (Catholic and Protestant) claim up to thirty-five million. More significant are the underground house churches which are said to have eighty or 100 million members. A description of revivals in China can be found in books such as *Jesus in Beijing* by David Aikman published by Monarch and *The Resurrection of the Chinese Church* by Tony Lambert published by Hodder and Stoughton.

In an essay with the title *The Next Forty Years for Christian Missions*[2] Patrick Johnstone shows that between 1960 and 2000 the balance between Western and and non-Western Christians changed dramatically. Whereas non-Western Christians formed only 35.5 percent of the whole in 1960 by 2000 this had changed to fifty-nine percent. If this trend continues, and the signs are that it will, then by 2040 seventy-five percent of Christendom will be non-Western.

It is in the detail of revivals that we obtain inspiration rather than in statistics. Therefore I will describe two twentieth-century revivals, the first in Korea and the second in Romania. Both these revivals as the details will show were characterized by deep repentance from sin. That feature is the most important part of revival. Indeed repentance which is deep and lasting is essential for a revival to be genuine. Repentance from sin is the heartland of revival.

There are many revivals which are on record and sadly many in which there has been failure in keeping records and descriptions.

I have chosen Korea and Romania because both of these revivals are ongoing. It is a feature of powerful biblically-based revivals that they do not fizzle out but go from strength to strength. It is generally agreed among historians of revival that the 1904 Welsh revival was a true revival but that there was a lamentable failure to conserve the positive gains because of a lack of Bible-based doctrine and too much stress on emotion.

Romania

Today, The Emanuel Baptist University of Oradea, is the only Baptist University campus on the continent of Europe. Its existence can be traced back to the revival which began in the Baptist Church in Oradea in 1974, a revival that can only be understood against a background of extreme persecution. The Communist Regime made an all-out attempt to stifle and ultimately destroy the witness of the church.

Life in socialist Romania was terrible. Under one of the most tyrannical régimes in Europe, food and energy shortages meant that many starved or froze to death. All dissent was suppressed. One in ten of the population was in the pay of the dreaded Securitate. Every telephone in the country was 'bugged'. People who tried to escape across the borders were shot. The churches were the special targets of the State system of repression and terror.

The official strategy was well thought out. The authorities focused a lot of attention on the leaders of the different denominations. Existing leaders were manipulated by bribery or threats, or were replaced by those who were more compliant or amenable. Priests and pastors of local churches were restricted in what they were allowed to do, and their preaching licences were withdrawn on the smallest pretext. Those who survived these attacks were further harassed by threats, smear tactics, physical assaults, and anything which would discourage them and hinder their effectiveness. Many were imprisoned or forced to leave the country. Of those who remained, all were 'encouraged' to inform on members of their congregations and an unknown number gave in to such pressure and became informers for the Securitate.

The way the Romanian Baptist churches fared is a good example of what happened to all Christian groups. Of the 1,196 Baptist churches and preaching stations, 532 were closed as 'unnecessary'. Of the 952 pastors, 787 lost their licences for 'irregularities'. Many of those who survived did so at the cost of their integrity. Only a few students were permitted to stay in the seminary in Bucharest, usually less than ten. Pastors were only permitted to preach in their own churches; they were not allowed to accept invitations to preach in other congregations. No evangelism, no children's work, no youth work, no special meetings for men or women, no charity work with church funds was permitted. Lists of church officers and potential officers had to be officially approved, as did the lists of baptismal candidates. Only children of Baptist parents could be baptized, all other baptisms were looked on as 'proselytising' of Orthodox members, which was illegal. In this one regard, the Orthodox views were accepted, and used, by the State authorities.

For three years before the revival began in the Second Baptist church of Oradea in 1974 a small group of five pastors met on Mondays for prayer. Josef Tson and Vasile Talos, both of whom stood courageously against the regime, were in this group. According to Vasile this prayer meeting explains all the amazing events that followed.

In the meantime Liviu Olah who had qualified as a lawyer before training as a pastor was called to be assistant pastor of the Second Baptist Church in Oradea in 1974. (The Hungarian Baptist Church is the First in Oradea). Olah had been debarred from the pulpit and spent much time in prayer and fasting. When he began his ministry he preached powerfully on the Great Judgement and on the reality of eternal hell. The church was in a very lethargic dispirited condition. There had been some distressing and scandalous incidents of drunken members.

Liviu Olah called for repentance. He began his sermons in a quiet tone. After about five minutes people were crying and under deep conviction of sin. They would call out for mercy. Those present spoke of 'divine power floating in the air'. The whole church seemed to be in tears. Those deeply burdened with sin came to the church. When they came to Christ they were filled with joy and would leave feeling that they were flying and not walking. Liviu preached evangelistic sermons clearly and powerfully. He did not confine his evangelistic preaching to Sunday services but preached at funerals and weddings when large numbers of unbelievers would be present.

By June 1974 over 100 converts had been baptized. In the next six months a further 249 were baptized. 149 were baptized in a single service.

The increase in numbers created a physical problem. The gallery began to crack under the weight of those cramming into it. In order to make room the side of the church was broken open to bring into view an area large enough to accommodate a further 800. This was achieved in spite of fierce opposition from the Communists who felt threatened by the gospel of hope which contradicted everything they stood for.

Liviu Olah's powerful preaching was allied to prayer — his own prayer life and also his insistence on intercessory prayer in the life of the church. Liviu Olah encouraged the members at Oradea to make the weekly church prayer meeting the very heart of the church's life. He emphasised fervency in prayer. He also urged believers to form prayer groups in homes in different parts of the town — something almost unheard of at that time!

He told people to draw up lists of relatives, friends, and workmates. He encouraged them to be very specific in praying for these people to be converted. He even suggested that they include the names of the local mayor and other Communist officials on their prayer lists! On one occasion a visitor asked Liviu Olah the 'secret' of the Revival. Olah turned to a child of eleven nearby and asked, 'How many people are on your daily prayer list?' The child replied, 'Eighty-six.' 'There is your answer! That is the reason for the Revival', said Olah.

The classical ingredients of revival, prayer and powerful preaching, were at the very centre of this spiritual awakening. A further part of the revival was profound repentance from sin. Liviu Olah's called for evidence of repentance. The saying developed, 'the repentance of the Repenters', the need for radical holiness.

Olah emphasized that as a holy God whose judgement is revealed against the sinfulness of unbelievers is also displeased with the sin and compromise in the lives of his people. He urged Christians to make a clean break with every known sin in their lives as individuals. But he went further and called on the Oradea church as a whole to make a stand on the need for absolute holiness.

The Second Baptist Church continued to grow and now has close to 4,000 members. A new contemporary style auditorium seating over 2,500 has been built. Adjacent is a new Baptist High School for 500 scholars. Twelve hectares of land have been provided for the Baptist University referred to above.

Korea

The Korean revival began in 1907 in North Korea and then spread across the whole nation. Tragically North Korea in the mid-twentieth century became the province of a ruthless atheistic and communistic regime. Christianity has been stamped out without mercy. How much has survived underground is unknown. The revival which began in 1907 did not continue with the same intensity but the fruit of it is seen is the growth of the church ever since, in the maintenance of daily early morning prayer meetings.

Writing in 1987 Dr Samuel H. Moffett, a retired veteran missionary in Korea, highlighted the fast growing church in that country.

When my father reached Seoul in 1890, there were between 10,000 and 17,000 Roman Catholics. Records for 1889 show that there were only seventy-four communicant Protestants. Forty years later when I was a boy in Korea in 1930, the number was 415,000 Christians, or two per cent of the population. When I returned in 1955 there were 1,117,000, or about five per cent. Very roughly that would mean one Korean or about twenty-three per cent. Approximately that would mean one Korean in a thousand was Christian in 1890, one in fifty in 1930, one in twenty in 1955 and one in four today.

The actual commencement of the revival can be traced back to special meetings that were organised in January in 1907. Information comes from an eye witness the Rev G. Lee and also from the testimony of Dr William Newton Blair a participant in the revival. The Banner of Truth published a descriptive work by Bruce Hunt in 1977 under the title *The Korean Pentecost*, 1977.

It was in January 1907 at Pyongyang in North Korea that there was a class for meetings for men. Some walked from ten to 100 miles to attend this series of meetings. 1,500 gathered. Missionaries and Korean pastors led the meetings. Dr Blair describes how the evening meeting was set aside for prayer.

After a short sermon, Mr Lee took charge of the meeting and called for prayers. So many began praying that Mr Lee said, 'If you want to pray like that all pray, and the whole audience began to cry out loud, all together. The effect was indescribable — not confusion, but a vast harmony of sound and spirit, a mingling together and of soul and spirit, a mingling together of soul moved by an irresistible impulse of prayer. The prayer sounded to me like the falling of many waters, an ocean of prayer beating against God's throne. It was not many, but one, born of one Spirit, lifted to one Father above. Just as on the day of Pentecost, they were all together in one place of one accord praying, and suddenly there came from heaven the sound as of the rushing of a mighty wind, and it filled the house where they were sitting.'

God is not always in the whirlwind, neither does he always speak in a still small voice. He came to us in Pyongyang that night with the sound of weeping. As the prayer continued a spirit of heaviness and sorrow for sin came down upon the audience. Over on one side, someone began to weep, and in a moment the whole audience was weeping.

Man after man would rise, confess his sins, break down and weep and then throw himself on the floor with his fists in perfect agony of conviction. My own cook tried to make a confession, broke down in the midst of it, and cried for me across the room: 'Pastor is there any hope for me, can I be forgiven?' and then threw himself on the floor and wept and almost screamed in agony.

Sometimes after a confession, the whole audience would break out in audible prayer, and the effect of that audience of hundreds of men praying together in audible prayer was something indescribable. Again after another confession they would break out in uncontrollable weeping and we would all weep, we could not help it. And so the meeting went on until two o'clock a.m. with confession and weeping and praying.

A few of us knew that there had been hatred in the hearts of some of the prominent men in the church, especially between a Mr Kang and a Mr Kim and we hoped that all would be confessed during these meetings. Monday night Mr Kang got the strength and told how he had hated Mr Kim and asked to be forgiven. It was wonderful to see that proud man break down and then control himself and then break down again as he tried to tell how he hated Mr Kim. When two o'clock came there were still men who had hated Mr Kim. When two o'clock came there were still men who wished to confess, but as the building was growing cold, and we still had another evening, we thought it best to close.

On the Tuesday evening the blessing continued as Dr Blair tells how events unfolded:

> We were aware that bad feeling existed between several of our church officers especially between a Mr Kang and Mr Kim. Mr Kang confessed his hatred between Mr Kim on Monday night, but Mr Kim was silent. At our noon prayer meeting several of us agreed to pray for Mr Kim. I was specially interested because Mr Kang was my assistant in the North Pyongyang Church and Mr Kim an elder in the Central Church and one of the officers in the Men's Association of which I was chairman.

As the evening meeting progressed I could see Mr Kim sitting with the elders behind the pulpit with his head down. Bowing where I sat I asked God to help him, and looking up saw him come forward. Holding to the pulpit he made his confession: 'I have been guilty of fighting against God. An elder in the church, I have been guilty of hating not only Kang You-Moon, but Pang Mok-sa (my Korean name).' I never had a greater surprise in my life. To think that this man, my associate in the Men's Association had been hating me without me knowing it! It seems that I had said something to him one day in the hurry of managing a school field-day exercise which gave offence, and he had not been able to forgive him. Turning to me he said, 'Can you forgive me, can you pray for me?' I stood up to and began to pray, 'Apa-ge, Apa-ge (Father, Father)' and got no further. It seemed as if the roof was was lifted from the building and the Spirit of God came down from heaven in a mighty avalanche of power upon us. I fell at Kim's side and wept and prayed as I had never prayed before. My last glimpse of the audience is photographed indelibly on my brain. Some threw themselves full length on the floor, hundreds stood with arms outstretched towards heaven. Every man forgot each other. Each was face to face with God. I can hear yet that fearful sound of hundreds of men pleading with God for life, for mercy. The cry went out over the city till the heathen were in consternation.

As soon as we were able we missionaries gathered at the platform and consulted. What shall we do? If we let them go on like this some will go crazy. Yet we dare not interfere. We had prayed to God for an outpouring of his Spirit upon our people and it had come. Separating we went down and tried to comfort the most distressed, pulling the agonised men to the floor and saying, 'Never mind brother, if you have sinned God will forgive you. Wait and an opportunity will be given to speak.'

Finally, Mr Lee started a hymn and quiet was restored during the singing. Then began a meeting the like of which I had never seen before, nor wish to see again unless in God's sight it is absolutely necessary. Every sin a human being can commit was publicly confessed that night. Pale and trembling with emotion, in agony of mind and body, guilty souls, standing in the white light of the judgement saw themselves as God saw them. Their sins rose up in all their vileness, till shame and grief and self loathing took complete possession; pride was driven out, the face of men forgotten. Looking up to heaven, to Jesus whom they had betrayed, they smote themselves and cried out with bitter wailing: 'Lord, cast us not away for ever!' Everything else was forgotten. Nothing else mattered. The scorn of men, the penalty of the law, even death itself seemed of small consequence if only God forgave. We may have our theories of the desirability or undesirability of public confession of sin. I had mine, but I know that when the Spirit of God falls upon guilty souls, there will be confession and no power on earth can stop it.

The Pyongyang class ended with the meeting on Tuesday night but the effects of the revival spread throughout the day.

On Wednesday morning there was the same manifestation at the advanced school for Girls and Women. Chapel began at ten o'clock. After a few remarks and prayer the girls broke down and began to weep and confess their sins, and until after twelve o'clock the meeting went on with nothing but prayer, tears and confession of sin. At the Central Church boy's school the same manifestation was present. On Thursday morning the Spirit fell on the primary school for girls. 'As some of us were going by the school room', says Mr Lee, 'we heard the sound of wailing and knew the same power was there'.

The revival spread to the country. The Christians returned to their homes in the country taking the Pentecostal fire with them. Everywhere the story was told the same Spirit flamed forth and spread till practically every church, not only in North Korea, but throughout the peninsula had received its share of blessing. In Pyongyang special meetings were held in various churches for more than a month. Even she schools had to lay aside lessons for days while the children wept out their wrongdoings together.

Repentance was by no means confined to confessions and tears. Peace waited upon reparation, whatever reparation was possible. The missionaries had their hearts torn again and again during those days by the return of little articles and money that had been stolen from them during the years. All through the city men were going from house to house, confessing to individuals they had injured, returning stolen property and money, not only to Christian but to heathen as well, till the whole city was stirred. A Chinese merchant was astonished to have a Christian walk in and pay him a large sum of money he had obtained unjustly years before.

This revival which spread through rural areas was remarkably free from fanaticism and excess.

These revivals remind us of the fact that Christ is keeping his promise when he said I will build my church and the gates of hell will not prevail against it. Revivals wherever they break out should stir us to prayer that we might be blessed with a mighty outpouring of the Holy Spirit.

*Practical
Considerations*

11. A call to prayer for revival

God is hiding his face from his people, and it is not an easy thing to seek his face. The Church today seems largely unwilling to face either of these realities. She insists on the one hand that God really is blessing her, and to prove it she cites all kinds of glowing statistics. But statistics never can measure the spiritual climate of the church ... A church can be bustling with activity and bursting at the seams and at the same time be infiltrated and permeated with the world's thinking and doing.

Sometimes the church does catch a glimpse of her desperate condition. But what is her response? All too often it has been to think that revival can come easily and quickly. We seek revival too casually and claim it too rapidly. Repentance is painstaking work. Glossing it over will never bring an extraordinary work of God.

These perceptive statements are made by Roger Ellsworth in his fifty-six-page paperback on revival, *Come Down, Lord.* He also makes this valuable observation: 'It appears that many Christians have just about given up on prayer. They retain it as a form to keep appearances up, but secretly they regard it as an exercise in futility.'

In response to these descriptions, I would point out that the first step in any revival is for the churches to come to a genuine sense of need. It is the work of the Holy Spirit to create a hunger and thirst for spiritual reality. He produces in believers a longing for powerful conversions. He also creates a holy discontent with their own lethargy and a dissatisfaction with the dead state of the church. This is a sensitive issue because it is easy to be self-righteous and critical. It is easy to blame the pastor or the preacher. It is also very common today to blame deadness in the churches on traditional forms of worship, as though sprucing up outward things will solve the problem. It is sometimes the case that bright forms of worship camouflage a dead spiritual condition, which, like putting make-up on a corpse, is merely cosmetic. When the Holy Spirit moves to create a deep desire for revival in the churches and awakening in society he does that from within, by stirring up a burden in the hearts of his people and prompting them to prayer.

Jonathan Edwards wrote in 1744 about God's dealings in a way that we would hope develop at this time, 'When he is about to bestow some great blessing on his Church, it is often his manner, in the first place, so to order things in his providence, as to show his Church their need of it, and to bring them into distress for want of it, and so put them upon crying earnestly to him for it.'[1]

It is my observation that there is a desire for revival ut very little specific intercession for the power of the Holy Spirit to return again in spiritual awakening. The prime obstacle that attends any attempt to organise a concert of prayer is that most pastors are engrossed with their responsibilities and simply do not have the time or energy for any extra concern.

In this call to prayer there are seven subjects which require our attention.

1. Is there really a biblical warrant for extraordinary prayer for revival?

Six reasons have been set out in chapters five through ten which urge that we should pray for revival. The optimistic interpretation of Scripture promises is not universally accepted even in reformed circles. Many doubt that there is really a warrant to pray for anything above the normal expectancy expressed in passages of Scripture like Psalm 126, namely, that those who sow can be assured of a harvest in due season.

I have pointed out many instances to show that revival is born in prayer. Prayer is the principal means of grace both personally and corporately. We are reminded by Zechariah 12:10 and Pentecost that prayer is an integral part of revival. The history of revivals shows that spiritual energy in the prayer meetings has invariably marked the beginning of revival.

The psalms provide us with examples of what it is to plead for revival:

Will you not revive us again,
    that your people may rejoice in you?

(Ps. 85:6).

Restore us, O God;
    make your face shine upon us,
that we may be saved

(Ps. 80:7).

Most prayers for revival recorded in the psalms spring from sorrow that the Lord's name is dishonoured because of the sad state of Zion. For instance, Asaph complains that there are no miraculous signs and no prophets left and that there is nobody who knows how long this weak state of defeat will last. Of particular concern is the mockery of the enemy:

How long will the enemy mock you, O God?
Will the foe revile your name for ever?

(Ps. 74:9-10).

There is an eloquent plea for revival recorded in Psalm 102. The psalmist declares the great love that the faithful have for the stones and dust of Zion. He refers to the destitute condition of those who pray (Ps. 102:17). This prayer is full of faith that the Lord 'will rebuild Zion and appear in his glory'.

Not only are there examples of prayer for revival but, as W. S. Plumer points out in his commentary on Psalm 80, 'God has filled our mouths with the most amazing arguments to be pleaded with him.'

'Let your hand rest on the man at your right hand, the son of man you have raised up for yourself. Then we will not turn away from you; revive us, and we will call on your name' (Ps. 80:17-18).

Special prayer by Daniel for restoration was accompanied by a penitent confession of sin (Dan. 9). His prayer is a model for us because it demonstrates the manner in which we should present our plight. Not all prayers for revival are in that mould. Psalm 44 is a lamentation describing desperate defeat and frustration. The psalmist does not confess particular sins. He pleads the fact that the people had been faithful; they had not strayed away. They had done all they could, but nevertheless experienced the bitter humiliation of defeat at the hands of their enemies. This psalm commends sincerity. It also displays desperate urgency:

> We are brought down to the dust;
> > our bodies cling to the ground.
> Rise up and help us;
> > redeem us because of your unfailing love
>
> > > > > (Ps. 44:8).

Pastors and missionaries have sometimes laboured faithfully for a lifetime with hardly any fruit. Their lives seem to have been wasted, their efforts futile. Not so, for in due time revival was sent from heaven even though the labourers did not live to see it. Quebec province, Canada, experienced remarkable revival during the 1980s. It has been noted that faithful pastors laboured for forty years preceding that time with seeming futility.

Possibly the greatest example of special prayer for revival is found in Isaiah from 63:15 right through chapter 64. The root cause of lack of revival is traced objectively to the sovereignty of God.

> Why, O Lord, do you make us wander from your ways
> and harden our hearts so we do not revere you?
>
> > > > > (Isa. 63:17).

The miserable situation is described: 'Our enemies have trampled down your sanctuary.' Most of all the Lord's glorious attributes of omnipotent power and tender compassion are pleaded with fervour. His absence is lamented. He is implored to come down and make his presence felt.

In the New Testament, the book of Acts in particular shows the centrality of corporate prayer. They were all together in one place prevailing in prayer when the Holy Spirit came down upon them (Acts 2:1-4). In every crisis the believers resorted to prayer (Acts 4:31; 12:5). Isn't spiritual apathy and powerlessness in a church a crisis which calls for prayer? Paul requested the prayers of the Thessalonians that the message of the Lord might spread rapidly and powerfully elsewhere, as it had done among them (2 Thess. 3:1-2; of 1 Thess. 1).[2] There can be no doubt that the churches at Ephesus and Laodicea were called to corporate prayer for revival following the sternness of the Lord's rebukes. In the case of Ephesus he complains that they have lost their first love and Laodicea is rebuked for the offence of lukewarmness.

There is, indeed, in times of special need and of the churches' weakness, a biblical warrant to resort to extraordinary prayer for revival.

2. What is our response if nothing happens?

In a lecture on the subject 'Prayer for revival', Alexander Cumming answers this question directly: 'When we persist in the exercise of prayer, notwithstanding all discouragement, we do honour to that loving-kindness which will not frustrate the anticipations that are formed upon the basis of his written declarations; and the longer the perseverance is maintained, and the more unpromising the symptoms against which it is upheld, the greater is the lustre reflected upon his character. Hence blessings of great magnitude are associated with ardour and perseverance in prayer; for the more splendidly these qualities shine, the greater is the attestation borne to his fidelity and love. It is the invariable constitution of the kingdom of heaven that blessings of great magnitude are not imparted except to prayers of the deepest urgency. When the disciples asked Jesus why they could not dispossess the demon he had ejected on his descent from the Mount of Transfiguration, he said to them, "This kind goeth not out but by prayer and fasting." This language intimated that, though the more common class might be easily expelled, that stubborn description could not be driven out except by great assiduity in supplication.'[3]

In dealing with the question of waiting in expectancy for our prayers to be answered, Edwards points out that every time we use the Lord's Prayer we are praying for his kingdom to be established on earth. 'Thus Christ teaches us that it becomes his disciples to seek this above all other things, that God would take to himself his reat power and reign and manifest his power and glory in the world.' Again, 'Every petition should be put up in subordination to the coming of God's kingdom and glory in the world.' Exhorting perseverance in prayer, he goes on, If we should continue some years, and nothing remarkable in providence should appear, we should act very unbecoming as believers, if we should therefore begin to be disheartened, and grow dull in seeking of God so great a mercy.' He then uses Micah 7:7 and Habakkuk 2:3-4 to show that our prayers are heard and will be answered in God's own time.[4]

Discouragement is a major factor used by Satan to hinder us in our prayers for revival. Those who feel isolated are particularly prone to the temptation of feeling that their prayers are useless. What can one person do? Edwards is most helpful when he emphasizes the value of the humblest believer. He says, 'There is no way that Christians in a private capacity can do so much to promote the work of God and advance the kingdom of Christ, as by prayer. Let persons in other respects be never so weak, and never so mean, and under never so poor advantages to do much for Christ and the souls of men; yet if they have much of the spirit of grace and supplication, in this way they may have power with him who is infinite in power and has the government of the whole world. A poor man in his cottage may have a blessed influence all over the world.'[5]

3. The importance of relating prayer for revival to all church endeavours

At all costs we must not fall into the error of thinking that the absence of revival is an excuse to discontinue our active evangelistic and missionary endeavours. The task of local and worldwide evangelism is mandatory and unceasing. Jesus promises to be with us in our efforts until the end of the world, revival or no revival!

The notion that nothing worthwhile can be done until revival comes can lead to the worst kind of lethargy. That is a trap to be avoided at all costs. It cannot be stressed enough that all prayer for revival must be accompanied by faithfulness in fulfilling the commission, which is binding upon us all, to reach everyone as effectively as we can with the gospel.

Evangelism

It is those who labour hard in evangelism who are able to pray most fervently for revival. This point is well illustrated by the life of David Brainerd described in chapter four. Brainerd describes how he agonized over the Indians among whom he laboured and how he often despaired that there would ever be a converting work among a people so darkened and depraved by sin. He worked and prayed on until he was favoured with a revival of astonishing power among the Indians.

Brainerd believed in the total helplessness of man in sin, the depravity of the fallen human will and the sovereignty of God in salvation. The practical implications of these truths could hardly have been more powerfully experienced in his life and ministry. What seems impossible with man is possible with God. When he saves, it is to the praise of the glory of his grace. Revival illustrates this decisively. Revival should be the passion of those who claim to believe in the doctrines of grace because, in a very clear way, the glory of salvation is ascribed to the triune God. We are required to labour and set the wood on the altar, but only the divine fire can come down and consume the offering. We are obliged to evangelize to the fullest possible extent, but only God can give the harvest (Ps. 126).

Open-air preaching and house-to-house visiting, more than anything else, have impressed on me personally the urgent need of revival. As shown in the chapter on decline there hs been an increasing indifference to spiritual realities among non-churchgoers in England. The voice of the church has little or no credibility for them. When I began my pastoral ministry in 1962, response to house-to house visiting was marked. That method, with which we must certainly persevere, seems to produce very little fruit now, but a little is better than nothing. Other pastors endorse the fact that there has been a steady overall hardening towards the gospel. Nevertheless there are some encouraging instances of many being brought to faith by evangelistic endeavour, often in deprived inner-city areas. Also from some churches, families are being reached by means of a variety of efforts aimed at different age groups.

Reformation

There is a saying that 'A Reformed church must always be reforming.' We can never be complacent about reformation. At local church level there is the question of discipline. When standards for church membership decline it is possible for churches to become mainly nominal, with only a small remnant of believers.

Then, more widely, it cannot be assumed that all preachers are committed to a faithful proclamation of the whole counsel of God's Word. Following the overwhelming tide of liberalism which has swept over most of the major Christian denominations and seminaries in the last 150 years, the gospel is missing in many churches. Revival results in a great love for the truth, leading to a desire to promote reformation in the churches and conform them to the standards set out in the New Testament. In the sixteenth century, a rediscovery of the gospel resulted in great numbers of conversions.

Some have tended to suppose that reformation is the automatic precursor of revival. That is not the case. It is always our duty to hold to the Scriptures as faithfully as we can. However, it does not follow that revival will necessarily result. Revival is God's prerogative. Yet reformation and revival are closely connected. In our efforts to advance reformation we should always pray that the Holy Spirit will, at the same time, use the truth to bring revival to God's people. Truth is a living thing. We are not concerned for the mere letter of God's Word but a desire to experience the power of it. As Paul, in writing to the Thessalonians said, 'Our gospel came to you not simply with words, but also with power, with the Holy Spirit and with deep conviction' (1 Thess. 1:5).

The need for powerful preaching

If we are praying for revival then we ought to expect the answers to our prayers to be evidenced in powerful Spirit-filled preaching. What kind of preaching is used by the Holy Spirit in an awakening? Certainly the history of revivals shows that the character of the preaching used is of the same kind and substance as that of Jesus and his apostles. It is preaching which embraces the central truths of the Bible, the trinitarian nature of God and his sovereign rule and purpose in this world. It will be preaching which explains man's ruin by the Fall, the appalling nature and consequences of sin and the necessity of repentance towards God and faith in the Lord Jesus Christ. The terrors of the law, the holiness of God and the reality of eternal hell have always been basic in revival preaching, as has the all-sufficiency of Christ's propitiation.

If ignorant sinners are to be awakened, principal biblical erms like justification, sanctification, regeneration and resurrection need to be made comprehensible to them in present-day language. Two of the greatest ever preachers of revival times were George Whitefield and Daniel Rowlands of Wales. Both men were able to weave all the above themes around any biblical subject in a fresh and powerful way.

Prayer for revival is a constant reminder of our desperate need for the mighty power of the Holy Spirit in preaching. There must be the material in our preaching which can be taken and used by the Holy Spirit to convince men of their sin, of their need of imputed righteousness and of the reality of judgement to come. Substance for preaching is gained by hard work. That is one factor. The other is prayer by which the power of the Holy Spirit is sought. As Paul says to the Corinthians, 'My preaching ... [was] with a demonstration of the Spirit's power'(1 Cor. 2:1-4). All ministers are to some extent or other involved in administration, which tends to take up their time so that they are hindered in their main work. When this danger threatened the apostles they declared: 'We will turn this responsibility over to [the deacons] and we will give our attention to prayer and the ministry of the word' (Acts 6:3-4).

Practical support of missionary endeavour

We saw in our consideration of Romans 11 that we should be thinking in international terms and of the church of Christ worldwide. Reports of revival in one country renew and strengthen the prayers and vision of God's people in other nations.

When we are personally involved in supporting missionaries to other countries, our vision is greatly widened and our appreciation of the glorious body of Christ enlarged. Praying for revival takes on a new meaning when we are personally involved with Christian workers in several different nations.

The relief of sister churches in oppressed countries

Church unity is illustrated in the New Testament by the way financial support was gathered from the Gentile churches to help alleviate the needs of the church in Jerusalem (1 Cor. 16:1-4). There is ample opportunity for well-placed churches to share with needy ones all over the world. The changed situation in Eastern Europe has lifted the restrictions regarding Christian literature, and there is urgency for Western churches to seek to meet the crying need for expository material, as well as for basic medical supplies, food and clothing in impoverished countries like Romania.

What has help given to churches in need to do with revival? Let us turn to Isaiah once more. He links the pouring out of the Holy Spirit to serious attention being given to the dual responsibilities of turning away from sins and attending to the needs of the oppressed and hungry (Isa. 58:9-14).

4. The importance of Christian unity and acknowledging the work of others

According to our Lord's high-priestly prayer recorded in John chapter 17, the unity of all those who are born again is of the same exalted kind as the unity of the three persons of the Godhead. He prays that 'all of them may be one, Father, just as you are in me and I am in you' (John 17:21). A very high value is placed on unity here. Psalm 133 declares that where unity is, 'There the Lord bestows his blessing, even life for evermore.'

Needless to say, this unity includes an experimental common enjoyment of the Trinity through the truth as expressed by Paul in Ephesians 4:1-6. It is a unity based on the truth and not a unity apart from the truth. Sharing this ground, we must be ready, when we pray for revival, to join with all who have the same burden whatever their denomination. We should acknowledge the efforts made in the quest for revival by groupings other than our own.

Jim van Zyl, writing in the magazine *Reformation Today* in 1972 on the subject of 'Obstacles to Revival', issued this challenge: 'Think of the last fifty years. Consider all the meetings, conventions and campaigns that have been organized. Honesty demands that we admit that only a very small proportion have had anything to do with the subject or need of revival. We have yet to see a major conference where evangelicals will gather and deliberately spend time inter-ceding for a new worldwide outpouring of the Spirit.'[6]

The Carey Conference which began in 1970 embraced the subject of revival for the first time in 1990, twenty years later! This neglect is surprising, since the emphasis placed on the almightiness of God's free and sovereign grace and on the omnipotence of od and his sovereignty by the Reformed constituency should logically lead to a quest for revival, and more concern to use the means of grace provided to seek one. Perhaps the struggle to regain the doctrines of grace has been so demanding that this emphasis on revival has been lost sight of.

But not all have been guilty of neglecting this subject. A few have written useful books on revival. We have only to scan the catalogues of publishing houses like the Banner of Truth and

Evangelical Press to see that excellent books documenting revivals have been published. A very small minority of churches have established weekly prayer meetings for revival. Doubtless a number of individuals have prayed faithfully over many years for a divine visitation. Bernard Honeysett, a minister now deceased said at the Carey Ministers' Conference at Ripon, 1990, that he had prayed specifically for revival in our land for thirty years. Dr Martyn Lloyd-Jones was a passionate believer in revival and preached a series of twenty-four sermons on the subject at Westminster Chapel in 1959 in commemoration of the 1859 revival.[7]

In England the Fellowship for Revival (formerly Baptist Revival Fellowship), has for a number of years organized its annual conference around the theme of revival. The Baptist Revival Fellowship (BRF) began in 1938 when some evangelical pastors in London began to meet together under the leadership of Theo Bamber with a concern for the low spiritual state of their churches and a consequent longing for a visitation of God in revival. Since that time the fellowship has emphasized various elements considered to be preparatory to revival, such as doctrinal purity and personal renewal.

5. How to report a revival without grieving the Holy Spirit

Perhaps the greatest single obstacle to revival is the pride of man. The Lord will not share his glory with another.

> I am the Lord; that is my name!
> I will not give my glory to another
>   or my praise to idols
>   (Isa. 42:8).

Revival is the greatest proof of the reality, power and glory of God in our dispensation. The temptation for the instruments to steal some of that glory for themselves is lethal. God lives with those who are contrite and lowly in spirit (Isa. 57:15). They are the ones used by him. While it is a great help and encouragement to others to hear of blessing, those concerned often prefer to maintain a low profile.

The way in which revivals are reported in the earlier narratives of awakenings reveals cautious and discreet reporting. A good example of objective reporting which is encouraging to read comes from a John McDowell of New Jersey, USA. He writes as follows:

The subscriber was settled as pastor of this congregation December 1804. In August 1807, a powerful and extensive revival commenced. The first decisive evidence of the special presence and power of the Holy Spirit was on the Sabbath under a powerful sermon on prayer by the Rev. Dr Gideon Blackburn. A number were awakened that day; and new cases of conviction, and hopeful conversion, were for a considerable time occurring at almost every religious meeting. The special attention continued for about eighteen months, and the number added to the communion of the church as the fruits of this gracious work was about 120. The subjects of it were generally deeply exercised; and most of them continued for a considerable time in a state of distress, before they enjoyed the comforts of the hope of the gospel. This revival was the first I had ever seen; and it was a solemn situation for a young man, totally inexperienced in such scenes. It was general through the congregation, and in a few weeks extended into neighbouring congregations and passed from one to another, until in the course of the year, almost every congregation, in what was then the Presbytery of Jersey, was visited.

The next revival with which the Lord favoured my ministry visibly commenced in December 1812. It was on a communion Sabbath. There was nothing peculiarly arousing in the preaching. I was not expecting such an event; neither as far as I have ever discovered, was there any peculiar engagedness in prayer, or special desire or expectation on the part of the Christians. I saw nothing unusual in the appearance of the congregation; and it was not until after the services of the day were ended, when several called in deep distress to ask me what they should do to be saved, that I knew that the Lord was specially in this place. This was a day of such power, (though I knew it not at the time) that as many as thirty who afterwards joined the church were then first awakened. And it is a remarkable circumstance that the same powerful influence was experienced, on the same day, in both of the Presbyterian churches in the neighbouring town of Newark. It was also communion season in both those churches.

This revival continued about a year, and the number of persons added to the communion of this church as its fruits was about one hundred and ten. The subjects of this revival generally were deeply and long distressed, and in many instances, their distress affected their bodily frames. Frequently sobbing aloud was heard in our meetings, and in some instances, there was a universal trembling, and in others a privation of bodily strength, so that the subjects were not able to get home without help. In this respect the revival was different from any others which I have witnessed. I never dared to speak against this bodily agitation, lest I should be speaking against the Holy Ghost; but I never did anything to encourage it.[8]

6. What is the place of fasting?

After Jesus had cast the demon out of the epileptic boy, the disciples came to him in private and asked, 'Why couldn't we drive it out?' He replied, 'This kind can come out only by prayer' (Mark 9:29). Some manuscripts have 'prayer and fasting'. We are confronted here by the reality of spiritual power. The issue seems quite clear that spiritual power is connected with a disciplined life of prayer and that the life of prayer can be strengthened by fasting. What effect does abstinence from food have on prayer? We can perhaps answer that question by asking another: why did Jesus fast for forty days? Was it to ensure complete spiritual power in preparation for his ministry which would involve the onslaught of Satan? We must always do full justice to the humanity of our Lord. At the end of his long fast he was hungry and physically

weak, yet he found it needful to undergo this severe discipline.
We note that Moses, in a time of supreme national and spiritual
need, also fasted for forty days. So did Elijah under exceptional
circumstances (1 Kings 19:8). When Daniel was deeply exercised
in his soul he fasted for twenty-one days (Dan. 10:2).

Every member of the nation of Israel knew about fasting because one day a year was set aside as a day of self-denial. This
was the Day of Atonement, which was the tenth day of the sev-
enth month. From the evening of the ninth day until the evening
of the tenth day was a time of abstinence from work and from
food. There were feast days but there was also this special day of
fasting which was regarded as synonymous with seeking the Lord
in humility.

There is no command to fast in the New Testament although
our Lord seems to take it for granted that the practice would continue. He said, 'When you fast, do not look sombre as the hypo-
crites do, for they disfigure their faces to show men they are fasting. I tell you the truth, they have received their reward in full. But
when you fast, put oil on your head and wash your face, so that
it will not be obvious to men that you are fasting, but only to your
Father, who is unseen; and your Father, who sees what is done in
secret, will reward you' (Matt. 6:16-18).

It is the subject of how we live in relationship with our heavenly Father that forms the context in which this teaching about
fasting is given. In our giving, praying and fasting we must not
be drawing attention to ourselves. It is not to impress others that
we fast. However, fasting was not a secret practice but something
participated in together. For instance, the church at Antioch was
worshipping the Lord and fasting when the Holy Spirit indicated
to them his will for Barnabas and Paul (Acts 13:2-3). Again the
members of the church at Antioch fasted and prayed when they
set these two men aside and sent them on their first missionary
journey. We note furthermore that when elders were appointed
thereafter in the newly planted churches, their ordinations were
accompanied by prayer and fasting.

We can conclude from the example of the churches in Acts
that whole churches can be involved in a voluntary exercise of
fasting. The occasion need not be confined to the setting aside of

pastors, elders and deacons. Fasting reinforces our earnestness in seeking God and is appropriate for any occasion of importance. In previous centuries days of prayer and fasting were set aside by churches or church associations at times of drought, or national danger or epidemic. It can be argued that if the pagan people of Nineveh, in response to the threat of judgement and destruction, humbled themselves and showed their earnestness by fasting, then how much more should we do so in a time of crisis? It is evident from the words of our Lord recorded in Matthew 12:41 that the repentance of the Ninevites represented a genuine turning to God. This will be seen in the coming judgement, when the example of those Ninevites will condemn the Jews who did not repent and turn to God when they were sent a greater preacher than Jonah.

A variety of reasons have disposed God's people to resort to prayer and fasting. In the case of Esther, Mordecai and the Jews, it was an extreme danger that motivated a solemn fast of no food or water for three days (Esth. 4:16). This action was in response to a desperate situation in which their lives were at stake.

Great difficulties were encountered when the Jews returned to Jerusalem. Under the leadership of Nehemiah they fasted and prayed and humbled themselves greatly before God. They expressed profound humiliation and sorrow for their sins (Neh. 9:1-3). It is obvious from the context that there was a great movement of the Spirit of God among the people at that time (Neh. 8:9-10). 2 Chronicles 20:1-4 tells of King Jehoshaphat. A vast army was approaching against Jerusalem. There was no way, humanly speaking, that Jehoshaphat could match such a military power. What did he do in his alarm? He proclaimed a great fast for all Judah. He then assembled the people of Jerusalem and led personally in a most fervent prayer. In answer to these petitions, reinforced with the earnestness of fasting, the Lord gave the nation a dramatic deliverance.

These examples indicate that when the Lord's people are vexed or perplexed or distressed, corporate prayer and fasting is a means of grace to which they should resort. As has been shown in this book, there are compelling reasons for the churches to seek the Lord for spiritual awakening. Nothing less than the powerful work of the Holy Spirit on a massive scale will meet the desperate spiritual poverty of our global age. The plight of the nations is desperate. A great awakening is massively overdue. The enemies of the gospel are winning the day in almost every area of the world. A colossal missionary work has yet to be achieved. If we have any jealousy at all for the name of our Lord Jesus Christ and his honour we will be willing to take extraordinary measures in interceding for a turning of the tide of defeat.

It would seem that the practice of fasting has disappeared in most evangelical circles. Yet as Dr Martyn Lloyd-Jones points out in an exposition of Matthew 6:16-18, 'The saints of God in all ages and in all places have not only believed in fasting, they have practised it.'[9] In the minutes of the Philadelphia Baptist Association, the manner of prayer and fasting is explained and reasons are suggested for the same: firstly, when impending judgement is feared; secondly, to intreat for revival and the spread of the Mediator's kingdom; thirdly, when there is a crisis in the church.[10] We can see this from the biographies and diaries from the past. For example, Andrew Fuller wrote in his diary on 11 May 1784, 'Devoted this day to prayer and fasting in conjunction with several other ministers.'

The warning of our Lord about the misuse of fasting should be carefully noted. From Isaiah 58 and Zechariah 7:4-7 it is clear that the Jews saw tremendous advantages in fasting as a means of grace, but they overpressed the practice into an arm-twisting exercise, as though they could thereby demand what they needed from God. In response to this overdoing of a valid means of grace the Lord made it clear that he was interested in the plight of those in slavery and of the poor and hungry, the homeless and destitute (Isa. 58:6-7). If the fast was accompanied by practical reformation then his glory would appear among them. During the captivity the Jews fasted and mourned regularly but here again their motives were questioned by Zechariah: 'Was it really for me that you fasted?' (Zech. 7:5). We need to watch our motives carefully. There are a few for whom the subject is dangerous because they do not eat enough anyway, and being spiritually zealous, can harm themselves. A much larger group, especially in prosperous countries, can secretly welcome the fasting concept because they are glad to use it as an occasion to lose weight. And so a mixed motive enters which beclouds the great central issue that in fasting and praying for revival we are seeking the person of the Lord. We are expressing our very real grief about our impoverished spiritual condition.

This is not the place to attempt a treatise on the subject of fasting. Others have done that.[11] But it is worth observing that organizations like Tear Fund link abstinence from food with giving to starving people in desperate situations. This seems to line up well with the concept of Isaiah 58:3-12:

> Is not this the kind of fasting I have chosen: to loose the chains of injustice...
> Is it not to share your food with the hungry...? Then your light will break forth like the dawn.

The strength of Tear Fund is that they do not divorce the practical from the spiritual. Of course we are to fast and pray, and give practically, and intercede for spiritual awakening. We must not set up one sphere at the expense of another.

7. What about a concert of prayer for the churches?

We have traced the beginning of the concept of the concert of prayer for revival and seen how it was developed by Jonathan Edwards in the treatise in which he made a strong appeal for the concert to be put into practice.

Information concerning the concert was spread by personal fellowship and private correspondence, not by a public organized campaign. In this way it found its way to those who were genuinely concerned and prepared to take action.

In the late eighteenth century some churches agreed to come together regularly on a regional basis for a day of fasting and prayer specifically for revival. This idea certainly warrants serious consideration and action.

The example of our predecessors encourages us as we seek to implement prayer for revival in our times.

Many rightly resist the multiplication of meetings, which can lead to the neglect of family and home responsibilities. If that is the case some time during the already existing prayer meeting could be structured to include intercession for revival. Alternatively it may be suitable to devote the first prayer meeting of every month to the subject of revival.

I recall attending a concert of prayer meeting held in First Baptist Church, Clinton, Louisiana, in which concerned pastors and church members from about eight churches came together for two and a half hours. The meeting was well led and structured as follows: hymn; Scripture verses and a brief historical sketch describing the legitimacy and usefulness of churches combining for prayer; silent prayer for personal revival; prayer for specific churches and impending events; prayer for the Islamic world; a final period of praise and thanksgiving.

Such meetings encourage unity and faith. Surely we stand in need of a rediscovery of the power of God in prayer, preaching and revival!

Bibliography — with comments

My primary purpose in this bibliography is to increase interest in revival. Therefore I have selected a few books which I deem to be the most helpful. Research students requiring a comprehensive bibliography are directed to a work by Richard Owen Roberts, *A Preliminary Bibliography of Published Books and Pamphlets on Revival*, Wheaton, 1982, which provides details for about 2,000 volumes. That is an overwhelming amount of material. Here I have chosen books which I deem most helpful and concentrated on those which are still in print or which might be more easily obtained from libraries. I especially commend the ministry of the Evangelical Library in London, 78A Chiltern Street, LONDON W1U 5HB.

First listed here are books about revival or which trace out the effects of revival and second books about the future.

Books about revival

Edwards, Jonathan. *Jonathan Edwards on Revival*. This volume contains one of Edwards' most analytical treatises on revival, *Distinguishing Marks of a Work of the Spirit of God*, and his famous *Narrative of Surprising Conversions*, a detailed account of the famous revival of religion at Northampton, Massachussets, in 1735. 168 pages, Banner of Truth. I recommend reading Edwards to those who are new to the subject of revival.

Edwards, Jonathan, *Thoughts on the New England Revival, Vindicating the Great Awakening*, Banner of Truth, 294 pages.

Edwards, Jonathan, *Praying Together for Revival*, edited by T. M. Moore. P and R., 204 pages, 2004. This book brings together the principal strands of Edwards' thinking on revival.

Edwards, Jonathan. 'An Humble Attempt to Promote Extraordinary Prayer', *Works*, vol. 2, pp.277ff.

Dallimore, Arnold. *The Life of George Whitefield* Two volumes. 612 and 620 pages. Banner of Truth. To travel with George Whitefield is to learn first hand what revival is.

Armstrong, John H. *When God Moves*. Harvest House Publishers. This highly commended book is comprehensive. Revival is well defined. Armstrong is acutely aware of the problem of revivalism and how that is confused with revival. He explains the impact of Charles Finney and rightly maintains that he was the principal person in bringing the change from God-sent revival to the idea that revival can be organised. Not all evangelicals adopted Finney's theology and methods but most did and that meant that the old views of revival were replaced by revivalism.

Davies, Ron E. *I Will Pour Out My Spirit. Monarch*, 285 pages, 1992. This work is excellent in quality and in its survey of revivals recorded in Scripture and through history right up to the mid 20th century.

Murray, Iain H. *Revival and Revivalism: the Making and Marring of American Evangelicalism 1750-1858*. Banner of Truth, 1994. This is a vitally important book as it describes with great clarity the transition from revival to revivalism.

Murray, Iain H., *Pentecost Today: The Biblical Basis for Understanding Revival*, Banner of Truth, 1998. Most encouraging is the fact that sometimes revival comes when there is great weakness and very few praying people. Iain Murray cites a number of notable instances of amazing powerful revivals coming down from heaven into situations of apathy, discouragement and weakness. pp.66ff.

Ortland, Raymond C., Jr., *Revival sent from God.* IVP, 2000. A
high quality book. Full of thoughtful material such as this, 'The
Lord Jesus may at any time and under any circumstances grant
us a fresh bestowment of his Spirit. And we can be certain that
nothing will defeat God's purpose whenever he chooses to renew
a season of unusual richness. How can any opposition down here
on earth restrain the outpouring of the Spirit from on high? ... At
any time, in any measure, upon any church, the Sovereign Lord
is able to send the showers of his Spirit, for his greater glory, our
richer joy, and the salvation of the nations.' page 93.

Cole, Richard W., Sr. *The Mighty Acts of God*, A Survey of Revival and Awakening in the United States of America. Revival Literature P. O. Box 6068, Asheville, NC 28816, USA. 250 pages.
This volume describes The Great Awakening (1740-1742), The
Second Awakening (1790-1814), The Third Awakening (1815-
1829), The Awakening of 1830, The Prayer Meeting Revival of
1858, the Awakening during the Civil War (1861-1865), and the
1905 Awakening.

Harman, Keith J. *Seasons of Refreshing: Evangelism and Revivals
in America.* Baker Book House. 300 pages, 1994. Harman tells
the story of evangelism in America from the early days of Freylin-
ghuysen through modern history to D L Moody, Billy Sunday and
Billy Graham. With Iain Murray's book and the work of Richard
Cole the reader will be able to trace out the metamorphism from
revival to revivalism.

Jenkins, T. Omri. *Five Minutes to Midnight: James Stewart and
Mission to Europe,* Evangelical Press, 121 pages, 1989. James
Stewart was just twenty-four years old when he traveled from Glasgow to what is now part of the USSR. He knew only the English
language but he had come believing that God had called him to
preach the gospel in Eastern Europe. Omri Jenkins tells this compelling story of an unknown evangelist, sent by God in answer to
prayer, whose labours over five years were attended with revival in
several countries up to the outbreak of the Second World War.

Cook, Paul E. G. *The Forgotten Revival.* Westminster Conference Paper, 1984. The period relates to Great Britain and the period is 1791 to 1830.

Evans, Eifion. *Fire in the Thatch.* Evangelical Press of Wales. 234 pages, 1996. Fifteen chapters on different revivals and aspects of revival.

Roberts, Richard Owen. *A History of Revivals in Scotland.* Published by International Awakening Press. 349 pages, 1995. Only goes up to 1860. Scotland has been noted for revivals in the 20th century.

Fish, Roy J. *When Heaven Touched Earth: The Awakening of 1858 and its Effects on Baptists.* Need to the Times Publishers, 342 pages, 1997.

Tyler, Bennett. *New England Revivals.* Richard Owen Roberts. 378 pages. 1980. Wonderfully inspiring descriptions of revival in which about 150 churches were visited in six years between 1797 and 1803.

Bradley, Joshua. *Accounts of Religious Revivals,* Richard Owen Roberts (publishers) 300 pages.

Bryant, David. *Concerts of Prayer: How Christians can Join together in Concerts of Prayer for Spiritual Awakening and World Evangelization, 162 pp.* Regal Books, 162 pages, 1984, revised 1988.

Edwards, Brian H. *Revival!: A people saturated with God,* 304 pages, Evangelical Press. The subject is presented in an arresting and readable manner structured under the headings, 'Before revival', 'During revival,' 'After revival' and 'Our response to revival'. You will enjoy this book!

Edwards, Brian H. *Can We Pray For Revival?* Evangelical Press, 213 pages, 2001.

Ellsworth, Roger. *Come Down, Lord!* 56 pages, Banner of Truth. A succinct, readable and biblically based treatment of the vital theme of revival. Its seven short chapters go directly to the heart of the matter, as their headings indicate: 'We Miss You, We Need You, We Wait for You, We Will Meet You, We Have Wronged You, We Belong to You, We Beseech You'.

Evans, Eifion. *Revival Comes to Wales: The Story of the 1859 Revival in Wales,* Evangelical Press of Wales, 123 pages.

Fish, Henry C., *Handbook of Revivals,* Gano Books, 424 pages.

Lloyd-Jones, D. Martyn. *Revival, Can We Make it Happen?* Marshall Pickering, 316 pages.

MacFarlan, D. *The Revivals of the Eighteenth Century, Particularly at Cambuslang,* 263 pp., Richard Owen Roberts.

Sprague, William B. *Lectures on Revivals.* Banner of Truth. This is two books in one. The first part of 260 pages consist of lectures on different aspects of revival. The second part of 165 pages is made up of eye witness descriptions of revival by well known leaders such as Archibald Alexander and Edward Payson.

Moore, Martin. *Boston Revival (1842),* Republished by Richard Owen Roberts, 148 pages.

Gillies, John, edited by H. Bonar. *Historical Collections of Accounts of Revival,* Banner of Truth. John Gillies, 560 pages. Scottish evangelical leader and friend and biographer of George Whitefield, was the first author to conceive the value of bringing the history of revivals together in one work. This large double-column volume contains a mine of information. It was originally published in 1754. Horatius Bonar edited the 1845 edition and supplemented it with additional material, including a valuable preface in which he writes, 'The world is still sleeping its "sleep of death". The volume before us contains not the history of the sleeping many, but of the waking few. Their story is as full of interest as it is of importance.

And when the voice of God awakes not one, but thousands, it may be in a day.'

Dallimore, Arnold. *The Life of Edward Irving: The Forerunner of the Charismatic Movement.* Banner of Truth, 185 pages, 1983.

Piper John. *A God Entranced Vision of All Things: The Legacy of Jonathan Edwards papers edited by John Piper and Justin Taylor. 286 pages, Crossway.* This is a book of papers published following the conference in Minneapolis attended by 2,500 to commemorate the birth of Jonathan Edwards (1703-1758). Especially commended is the chapter by J I Packer *The Glory of God and the Reviving of Religion: A Study in the Mind of Jonathan Edwards.*

Orr, Edwin. *The Flaming Tongue: The Impact of the 20th Century Revivals,* Moody Press, 241 pages, 1973. Beginning with the revival in Wales in 1904, the author de-scribes in twenty-five chapters revivals in many nations: the UK, Scandinavia, America, Brazil, Australia, New Zealand, South Africa, India, China, Korea and Japan. This is an important book because it presents complexities with regard to the analysis of the phenomena of revival. Increasingly the method of calling for decisions has come to prevail with the Arminian theology that goes with it. There is a need to discern between evangelistic campaigns and revivals that are not organized by men. Then too there is the rise this century of Pentecostalism and more recently of the charismatic movement. In spite of the difficulties that confront us, Edwin Orr makes a cogent case when he urges that the period 1904-1910 was a time of worldwide awakening. Few possess a knowledge of church history, and of revivals in particular, broad enough to be able to analyse the principles involved in revival. Those concerned with this subject will need to read this book.

Phillips, Thomas. *The Welsh Revival: Its Origin and Development,* Banner of Truth, 147 pages. The author was an eyewitness of much that he records. His concern is to show the marks of true Christianity in a time of revival and, pre-eminently, the moral change which is to be found in every true convert: 'They are told that excitement is no conversion and that whatever confidence they may have, it is a delusion unless it is accompanied by hatred of sin, and a renunciation of it in every shape and form.' The passage of time was to confirm the correctness of Phillips' early account of one of the most glorious years in Welsh and Christian history.

McGrath Alister, *Evangelicalism and the Future of Christianity*. IVP, 209 pages, 1995.

Jenkins, Philip, *The Next Christendom- The Coming of Global Christianity*, Oxford University Press, 269 pages, 2002. This is an unusual book inasmuch it is analysis of where Christianity is moving and what the situation will be in 2050. There is no serious attempt in this book to examine evangelicalism as an entity. Everything Christian is lumped together. Nevertheless it is an important book. Documented clearly is the fact that Christianity is dying is Western Europe but growing rapidly in China, much of Asia, in Latin American and in Africa. Jenkins observes that Christianity is flourishing among the poor and persecuted while it atrophies among the rich and secure. He concludes with these words of wisdom, 'Christianity is never as weak as it appears, nor as strong as it appears. And whether we look backward or forward in history, we can see that time and time again, Christianity demonstrates a breathtaking ability to transform weakness into strength.'

Johnstone, Patrick. *The Church Is Bigger Than You Think: The Unfinished Work of World Evangelisation.* Christian Focus. 314 pages. 1998. Unlike Jenkins Johnstone attempts to keep his eyes on Bible-believing (evangelical) Christianity and Pentecostal growth. He acknowledges the great difficulty involved (Page 109). A chapter is devoted to How can a local church become Mission-minded? This is a excellent companion to the handbook OPERATION WORLD (21ST Century Edition Patrick Johnstone and Jason Mandryk, Paternoster, 797 pages, 2001).

Johnstone Patrick. *The Next Forty years for Christian Missions.* This is a ten page essay which forms part of the book Global Passion edited by David Greenlee to commemorate the contribution of George Verwer to World Mission. Published in 2003 by Authentic Lifestyle.

Aikman David. *Jesus in Beijing: How Christianity is Transforming China and Changing the Global Balance of Power.* Monarch, 245 pages, 2005. If the present rate of conversion continues it is possible that in the next thirty years one third of the China's population could be Christians. The potential is enormous.

Lambert Tony. *The Resurrection of the Chinese Church.* Hodder and Stoughton 328 pages 1991. Included is a stirring chapter describing intense revival. This chapter reminds us of the supernatural sphere invading the natural. Does God perform healing miracles today? He does exactly as he pleases and his power is no different from that reported in the New Testament. However his agenda is not the same. The apostles attested the authenticity of the resurrection of Jesus and the authority of the New Testament. When miracles take place today they are to encourage his people and must never be used to endorse a sect or a new prophet. Also we have to contend with a massive amount of fraud by those who claim to perform healing miracles but use their ministries for financial gain.

Hefley, James & Marti. *By Their Blood: Christian Martyrs of the 20th Century,* 1979, reprinted 1988, 638 pages, Baker Book House. This volume, which comprehensively surveys Christian martyrdom in the 20th century, deserves the claim to be a continuation of Foxe's Book of Martyrs.

Hulse, Erroll. *Crisis Experiences,* Carey Publications, 138 pages. This book expounds the subject of the baptism of the Spirit. No specific experience of empowerment is commanded for believers in the New Testament. Nevertheless there are many experiences of empowerment, especially in times of revival, about which we need to be positive rather than negative.

Revival of Religion, The: Addresses by Scottish Evangelical Leaders Delivered in Glasgow in 1840, Banner of Truth, 468 pages.

Few things more stimulate interest in, and prayer for, a work of revival than the record of what God has done in the past, and the stories of the lives he has used. But alongside the history of revivals it is vital that we should understand the biblical principles of revival. Both may be found in this volume. The style of most of the writers is unfortunately verbose and may prove irritating to the reader. All that they have to say could be better expressed in half the space.

Books about the future (eschatology)

David, John Jefferson, *The Victory of Christ's Kingdom: An Introduction to Postmillennialism*, Canon Press, 94 pages, 1996. By far the best short treatment available.

Edwards, Jonathan, *The History of Redemption*, Banner of Truth, 450 pages. This classic work is included in volume one of the two volume edition of Edwards' works published by the Banner of Truth. This is an outstanding work when we consider the limitations in knowledge of the wider world that prevailed in the mid 18th century. Note the following, 'Then shall the many nations of Africa, the nations of the Negroes, and other heathens who chiefly fill that quarter of the world, who now seem to be in a state but little above the beasts, and in many respects much below them, be enlightened with glorious light, and be delivered from all their darkness, and shall become civil, Christian, understanding and holy people. Then shall the vast continent of America, which now in so great a part is covered with barbarous ignorance and cruelty, be everywhere covered with glorious gospel light and Christian love; and instead of worshipping the devil, as now they do they shall serve God, and praises shall be sung everywhere to the Lord Jesus Christ, the blessed Saviour of the world'.

Kik, J. Marcellus. *An Eschatology of Victory,* 268 pages, Presbyterian & Reformed. The author expounds Revelation chapter 20 verse by verse, and does the same with Matthew 24. This is an outstanding book an immense help to those who are confused about the Olivet discourse and perplexed about how to understand Revelation 20.

Brown, David. *Christ's Second Coming: Will it be Premillennial?* First published in 1983 and republished by Baker Book House in 1983, 500 pages, pure gold. This book should be kept in print.

Mathison, *Postmillennialism and Eschatology of Hope*, P&R, 286 pages, 1999.

Gentry, Kenneth L Jr., Editor *Thine is the Kingdom, Practical Postmillenialism*, Chalcedon, 260 pages. A variety of essays including chapters by Benjamin B. Warfield and J. A. Alexander.

Gentry, Kenneth L. Jr., *He Shall Have Dominion*, Institute for Christian Economics, 582 pages, 1992.

Murray, Iain. *The Puritan Hope,* 265 pages, Banner of Truth. This outstanding book describes how the promises of Scripture inspired pioneer missionary endeavour. Chapter eleven bears the title, The Eclipse of the Hope, and describes how the former more hopeful views of the future were engulfed by premillennial views during the 18th Century. The role of Edward Irving in this change is described (see book on Edward Irving by Arnold Dallimore).

Fairbairn, Patrick. *The Interpretation of Prophecy*, Banner of Truth, 528 pages, 1993.

Terry, Milton. *Biblical Hermeneutics*. Zondervan. 782 pages, eighth edition 1980.

Venema, Cornelis, P. *The Promise if the Future*, Banner of Truth, 535 pages, 2000.

Waldron Samuel E. *To Be Continued: Are the miraculous gifts for today.* Calvary Press Publishing, 116 pages, 2005. Comment by Phil Johnston in the preface reads, 'To claim that the spiritual gifts are still operative today is as spiritually dangerous as believing that the canon of Scripture is still open'. This book is commended to those who believe that revival depends on the restoration of the charismatic gifts.

Hulse, Erroll, *The Restoration of Israel*, Henry Walter, third edition, 192 pages,1982

Hulse, Erroll, *The Puritans and the Promises*, Westminster Conference Paper for 1999. The Reformed and Puritan view of the antichrist set forth.

Hill Charles E. *Regnum Caelorum: Patterns of Millennial Thought in Early Christianity*, Eerdmans, 315 pages, 2001. A fine scholarly work tracing out the story in the early centuries of chiliasm (taking Scriptures literally that ought to be taken symbolically or metaphorically). Chiliasm did eventually fall into disfavour and was for ages considered heterodox by the churches of East and West.

Notes

Introduction

1. Orr, J. Edwin, 'The Event of the Century'. The 1857-58 Awakening: a Startling Update. Unpublished ms, cited in Iain Murray, *Revival and Revivalism*, p.332.
2. Orr, J. Edwin, *The Light of the Nations*, Paternoster, p.109.
3. Fish, Roy J., *When Heaven Touched Earth, The Awakening of 1858 and its Effects on Baptists*, Need of the Times Publishers, 1996, p.46.
4. Orr, *The Light of the Nations*, p.105.
5. Fish, *When Heaven Touched Earth*, p.43.
6. Orr, *The Light of the Nations*, p.116.
7. Roy J.Fish, *When Heaven Touched Earth*, and Edwin Orr, *The Light of the Nations*, provide detailed descriptions of the spread of the revival.
8. Phillips, Thomas, *Welsh Revival: Its Origin and Development*, Banner of Truth, 1995.
9. The Presbyterian Magazine. USA vol. 8, 1858.
10. The Presbyterian Magazine. USA vol. 8, 1858.
11. Blackburn, George A. ed, *The Life and Work of John L. Girardeau*, Columbia, SC, 1916.
12. Orr, J. Edwin, *The Light of the Nations*, Paternoster, 1965, p.126ff.
13. Orr, J. Edwin, *The Flaming Tongue — The Impact of the 20th Century Revivals*, Moody Press, 1973. pp.116ff.

Chapter 1

1. The Puritan Conference papers have been reprinted by Presbyterian and Reformed Publishing. See volume 1 (1956-1959) for Lloyd-Jones's speech.
2. Buchanan, James, *The Office and Work of the Holy Spirit*, 1966, Banner of Truth.
3. All statistics in this chapter are taken from Patrick Johnstone, *Operation World: When We Pray God Works*, Gabriel Resources, 2001.
4. Edwards, Jonathan, *Works*, Banner of Truth, vol. 1, p.348.
5. Cited from the *Banner of Truth* magazine, no. 185, from the second of two articles by Iain Murray with the title 'Necessary Ingredients of a Biblical Revival'. The first articles appeared in *Banner of Truth*, no. 184.
6. Edwards, *Works*, vol. 1., p.348.
7. Edwards, Jonathan, *The Religious Affections*, Banner of Truth, 1961, p.192.
8. Logan, Samuel T., Jr., *Preaching*, Evangelical Press, 1986, p.369.
9. Ibid., pp.62-90.
10. For a further discussion of the words 'renewal' or 'revival' see Richard Lovelace, *Dynamics of Spiritual Life: An Evangelical Theology of Renewal*, IVP, 1979.
11. Murray, Iain H., *D. Martyn Lloyd-Jones: The first 40 years, 1899-1939*, Banner of Truth, 1982, pp.203ff.

Chapter 3

1. Flavel, John, *The Mystery of Providence*, Banner of Truth, 1976, p.158.
2. Bacon, Francis, *The Essays*, Penguin, p.203.
3. See *The Puritan Papers, vol. 2: 1960-1962*, Presbyterian and Reformed.
4. Edwards, Jonathan, 'The End for Which God Created the World'.
5. Edwards, Jonathan, 'Thoughts on Revival', *Works*, vol. 1., pp.398ff.

6. Edwards, Jonathan, *Charity and Its Fruits*, Banner of Truth, 1969.
7. Edwards, 'Thoughts on Revival', p.426.
8. Piper, John and Justin Taylor, *God Entranced Vision of All Things: The Legacy of Jonathan Edwards*, Crossway Books, pp.100-101.
9. Ibid., pp.101-104.
10. Ibid., p.112.
11. Ibid., p.24.
12. Cited in J. Edwin Orr, *The Second Evangelical Awakening*, p.110.

Chapter 4

1. Warfield, B. B., *Counterfeit Miracles*, Banner of Truth. Eerdmans published this book in 1954 with the title *Miracles, Yesterday and Today*. Present-day claims to charismatic gifts resemble very much the Irvingite movement brilliantly described and analysed by Warfield.
2. John Sott's commentary *The Message of Acts: The Spirit, the Church, and the World* is a solid commentary on the movement of the Spirit in modern times.
3. For details of the revival among the Indians, as well as the source for quotations, see *The Life of David Brainerd*, Baker Book House, 1978.

Chapter 5

1. Philips, Thomas, *The Welsh Revival*, Banner of Truth, pp.

Chapter 6

1. Roberts, Richard Owen, *The Solemn Assembly*, a fifteen-page booklet published by International Awakening Press, USA.
2. Lescelius, Robert. 'Revival and the History of the Church,' *Reformation Today*, Issue 113.
3. Edwards, Brian H., *Revival: A People Saturated with God*, EP, 1990.

4. Lohse, Bernard, *Martin Luther*, T & T Clark, Edinburgh, p.11.
5. Estep, William R., *Renaissance and Reformation*, Eerdmans & Paternoster, p.45.
6. Schwiebort, Ernest G., *Luther and his Times*, Concordia, p.605.

Chapter 7

1. This account was documented by Dr Jack Allen of the Dutch Reformed Church (NG) in a paper given at the annual Evangelical and Reformed conference at Skogheim in Natal.
2. Bradley, Joshua, *Accounts of Religious Revivals in many parts of the United States from 1815 to 1818*, Richard Owen Roberts Publishers, pp.145ff.
3. Fawcett, Arthur, *The Cambuslang Revival*, Banner of Truth, 1971, pp.223ff.
4. The description of Sutcliff's role is cited from Reformation Today, issue 104, 'How can we pray and work for Worldwide Revival?' by Michael Haykin.
5. The description of the revival in Bala and the references to William Bramwell have been taken from the address given by Paul Cook at the Carey Conference for ministers, Ripon, 1990.
6. Tucker, Ruth A. *From Jerusalem to Irian Jaya: A Biographical History of Christian Missions*, Zondervan, 1983, p.70.
7. Johnstone, Patrick, *Operation World*, STL, 1986.

Chapter 8

1. J J Murray in *Where is God now Gone. The Present State of Church and Nation*. Free Church of Scotland (Continuing) 2003
2. Hitchins, Peter, *The Abolition of Britain: From Lady Chatterley to Tony Blair*, Quartet, 1999, pp.177ff.
3. ibid page 185.
4. J J Murray, ibid p.7.
5. *The Churchman*, Summer 2005.
6. Documentation for crime and prison population can be found on www.reform.co.uk.

Chapter 9

1. Edwards, Jonathan, *Works*, vol. 2, p.280.
2. Edwards, Jonathan, *The Distinguishing Marks of a Work of the Spirit of God*, Banner of Truth, p.89.
3. *Lectures on Revival by Ministers of Scotland*, Banner of Truth, p.188.
4. Ibid., p.204.
5. *Banner of Truth*, Issue 304, January 1989.
6. Iain Murray, *The Puritan Hope*, Banner of Truth; Erroll Hulse, *The Restoration of Israel*, Carey Publications.
7. Louis Berkhof, Herman Hoeksema, William Hendriksen, Hendrik Krabbendam — not every expositor of the Dutch extraction is in this school, Gisbertus Voetsius (1589-1676) is an exception!
8. Elnathan Parr (1651), Charles Hodge, Robert Haldane, Sanday and Headlam, John Brown, H. G. C. Moule, W. G. T. Shedd, David Brown, Albert Barnes, F. F. Bruce, C. E. B. Cranfield and Leon Morris.
9. Godet, Frederick Louis, *Commentary on Romans*, Kregel, p.416.
10. *Banner of Truth*, issue 304, Jan. 1989.

Chapter 10

1. Jenkins, T. Omri, *Five Minutes to Midnight*, pp.15-17.
2. *Global Passion,* a book of essays to mark the George Verwer's contribution to World Mission, Authentic Lifestyle, 2003.

Chapter 11

1. Edwards, Jonathan, 'Thoughts on Revival', *Works,* vol. 1, p.426.
2. Michael A. G. Haykin explores the New Testament data in his article 'Praying for Revival: is it Biblical?' *Reformation Today*, issue 115.
3. *The Revival of Religion, Addresses by Scottish Evangelical Leaders delivered in Glasgow in 1840*, Banner of Truth, p.134.
4. Edwards, Jonathan, 'A Call to United Extraordinary Prayer',

Works, vol. 2, pp. 291-312.
5. Edwards, Jonathan, 'Thoughts on the Revival', *Works*, vol. 1, p.426.
6. *Reformation Today*, issue 13, 1972.
7. Martyn Lloyd-Jones, *Revival: Can we make it happen?*, Marshall Pickering, 1986, 316pp.
8. Sprague, William, *Lectures on Revivals*, Banner of Truth, p.62.
9. Lloyd-Jones, Martyn, *Sermon on the Mount*, IVP, 1960, vol. 2, p.36.
10. *Minutes of the Philadelphia Baptist Association*, reprinted by Baptist Book Trust, (USA), 1976, p.167.
11. See Calvin's *Institutes*, Book 4, sections 14-20. David Rushworth Smith, Fasting, New Wine Press, 1988.

Index

Symbols

1858 revival 7
1859 revival 93-94
1859 Welsh revival 10, 76
1904 Welsh revival 91, 133, 135

A

Aberavon 30
Aberdeen 77
Abraham 83, 121, 129
Acts, book of 55-58
Aikman, David 134
Alexander, James W. 8
Anglicans 103
Anglican Church 110
Anglo-Catholic 28
Antioch 159
Arnold of Brescia 87
Asa 82
Asaph 110
Asia Minor 56
Assemblies of God 20
Atonement, Day of 159
Awakening 17-34
Awakening, the Great 24-25, 81, 91, 94
Awakening, the Second 62, 91, 94
Awakening, the Third 91

B

Bablyon 85-86, 122, 130
Bacon, Francis 42
Baker, Daniel 11
Bala 101, 134, 172, 180

Ballemena 12
Bamber, Theo 156
Banner of Truth Trust 10-11, 17, 28, 130, 138, 155
baptism 55, 58, 61, 64, 136
Baptist, John the 61
Baptist churches of the Northamptonshire Association 97
Baptist Revival Fellowship 156
Baptist Union 110. 113
Baptists 26, 97-98, 100, 113
Baptists, Grace 110, 114
Baptists, Particular 98, 100
Baptists, Reformed 100, 114
Baxter, Richard 91
Berlin wall 127
Bethel 21, 86
biblical theology 83
Blackburn, Gideon 157
Blair, William Newton 138
Boer War 13
Bokim 84
Boston U.S.A. 10, 26
Bourne, Hugh 99
Brainerd, David 19, 41-43, 49, 66-69, 151
Bramwell, William 102
Brehaut, Walter 29
Brethren of the Common Life 88
Britain 10, 28, 74, 93-94, 99, 105, 109, 111, 115-116
Buchanan, James 19
Bucharest 136
Budgen, Victor 45

C

Calvin, John 90
Calvinistic Methodists 100
Cambuslang 96
Cameron, David 106
Canada 148

Carey, William 97
Carey Conference 94, 155
Carey Ministers' Conference 156
Cele, John 88
Center, World Prayer 31
Chaldeans 129
charismatic movement 17, 21
Charismatic renewal 28, 31
charismatic revivals 31
*Charismatics and the Word of
        God* 45
Charity and Its Fruits 17, 45
Charles, Thomas 101-102
Chicago 10
Chilton, David 37
China 134
Church of England 51, 110-111
Church of Scotland 112
Civil Partnership Act 107
Columba 87
Columbia Theological Seminary
        11
Colville, Mrs 12
Come Down, Lord 145
Communion 157-158
Congregationalists 100
Constantine 87
conviction of sin 9, 12, 17, 21,
        23, 43, 49, 60, 64-66, 98,
        101, 136, 139, 153, 157
Cook, Paul 94, 99
Corinth 11, 33, 40, 66
Counter-Reformation 90
Cromwell, Oliver 88
Cumming, Alexander 149

D

Dallimore, Arnold 17
Daniel 38, 54, 79, 86, 130, 148,
        153, 159
David 9, 81, 83, 126

Davidson, John 96
Davis, David 106
Derbe 19
Devotio Moderna 87-88
discouragement 36, 149-150
dispensationalism 30
*Distinguishing Marks of a Work of
        the Spirit of God, The* 24,
        43
Doddridge, Philip 100
Dorothea Mission 103
Downgrade Controversy 113
Dutch Reformed Church 8, 14,
        93

E

East Timor 20
Eastern Europe 29, 32, 127, 154
Ecumenical renewal 18
Edinburgh 77
Edwards, Brian 83
Edwards, Jonathan 17, 22, 23,
        24, 25, 41, 53, 75, 81, 91,
        95, 102, 119, 120, 121,
        146, 150
Elijah 34, 159
Ellsworth, Roger 145
Emanuel Baptist University 135
Ephesus 19, 55-66, 78, 149
Erskine, John 97
Esther 160
Ethiopia 25-26
European Union 105
*Evaluation of Claims to the Char-
        ismatic Gifts, An* 45
Evangelism 19, 79, 114, 136,
        151, 167
Exodus 20, 81, 85
Ezekiel 9, 34, 36, 38, 46, 58, 65,
        122
Ezra 79, 82, 84

F

Fairclough, Samuel 91
faith 23-25
faith healing 54
fasting 27, 46-47, 75, 79, 85-86, 94, 96, 136, 150, 158-162
Fellowship for Revival 156
Fetler, William 133, 184, 186
financial support 154
FIEC 114
First Baptist Church, Clinton, Louisiana 163
First London Confession of Faith 60
Fish, Roy J. 8
Five Minutes to Midnight 133
Flavel, John 41
Forgotten Revival, the 25, 94, 99
France 87, 90, 105, 115
Frederick the Wise 89
Fuller, Andrew 161

G

Geneva 90
Geneva Company of Pastors 90
Gentiles 11, 55, 58, 123-124, 130-131
Girardeau, John L. 11, 12
Glasgow 77
Godet, Frederic 131
Grace Baptists 110
Great Awakening 91
Great Commission 54
Groote, Gerhard 88
Guernsey 29

H

Habakkuk 129, 150
Hagar 129
Hannah 85

Haykin, Michael 98
Hebrews 34, 39, 57
Hebrides 91
Hegius, Alexander 88
hell 22, 59, 63-64, 68, 136, 142
Hendriksen, William 37, 39
Herrnhut 102
Hezekiah 82-83
History of the Work of Redemption, A 43, 81
Hitchins, Peter 107
Holiness of God 21, 59-60, 66, 134, 153
Holland 88
Honeysett, Bernard 156
House churches 134
Humble Attempt to Promote Extraordinary Prayer, An 95, 97, 119
Humility 35, 44, 74, 86, 159
Hus, Jan 87

I

Independents 100
India 13, 26
Indians (North American) 19, 41-43, 49, 66, 68-69, 151
Indonesia 46
Ireland 12, 77, 116
Irving, Edward 17, 54
Islam 116
Islamic nations 37, 127, 163
Italy 40. 87-88. 90. 105

J

Jacob 21, 85, 122-123
Jehoiada 82
Jehoshaphat 82, 160
Jehovah's Witnesses 40, 110, 115

Jenkins, T. Omri 133
Jeremiah 29, 82, 86
Jerome 87
Jersey, Presbytery of 157
Jesus in Beijing 134
Joel 33, 58, 82
John the Baptist 61, 87
Johnstone, Patrick 103, 134
Joshua 66, 130
Josiah 82
Judah 82-83, 160
Judisch, Douglas 45
justification 12, 33, 42, 59, 64,
      89, 153

K

Keddington 91
Kelly, Douglas 11
Kidderminster 91

L

Laodicea 78, 149
Lambert, Tony 134
Lang, John 89
Lanphier, Jeremiah 8
Latvia 133
Legitimacy Act 107
Lescelius, Robert 81-82
Leupold, H. C. 124-125
Livingstone, John 58
Lloyd-Jones, D. Martyn 18, 30,
      156
London Confession of Faith 60
Lorimer, John G. 122
Lord's Prayer, the 150
Lovelace, Richard 98
Luther, Martin 89
Lyons 87

M

Mariorat, Augustin 90
Martyr, Peter 90
McDowell, John 157
McQuilkin, James 12
Melanchthon, Philip 89
Methodist revival 94
Methodists 62, 97, 112
Methodists, Calvinistic 100
Methodists, Primitive 99-100
Methodists, Weslyan 99, 102
Metropolitan Theatre 10
Ministries, Global Harvest 31
miracles 17, 45, 53-54, 56-57
Miracles Yesterday and Today 54
miraculous signs 53
Moffett, Samuel H. 138
Moravia 102
Moravians 103
Mormons 110, 115
Moule, Handley 50
Murray, Andrew 103
Murray, John J. 108

N

*Narrative of Surprising Conver-
      sions, A* 22, 43
Native Americans 11, 66
Nehemiah 79, 82, 84, 160
Nepal 20
New England 25, 42-44, 95
New Frontiers 17
New York 8, 9
Newark 158
Nicodemus 62
Nineveh 160
Northampton, U. S. A. 22-23,
      41-43
Northamptonshire Association
      97-98
North Dutch Church 8

O

Olah, Liviu 136, 137
Olney 97
Operation World 47, 103, 105
opposition 55-56
Oradea 135-138
Orr, Edwin 7, 19
Osborne, Grant R. 37
Otis, eorge 30
Owen, John 53, 91

P

Packer, J. I. 43, 48
Palmer, Benjamin Morgan 11
Particular Baptists 97, 98-100
Payson, Edward 22
Pentecost 8, 20, 55, 61, 66, 93
Pentecostals 110, 114
Peter of Bruys 87
Peterson, Dennis 108, 111
Pharaoh 85
Philadelphia 9
Piper, John 50
Pope Urban VI 88
pornography 107
Postmodernism 106
prayer 38, 79, 95, 120, 121, 146, 151, 162
prayer meeting 9
Prayer meetings 10
prayer meetings 7, 35, 75
Primitive Methodists 100
promises of God 129
Puritan 28, 42
Puritan Conference 18, 43
Puritans 53, 90

Q

Quebec 148

R

Reformation, The 28, 87, 89, 152
Reformation Today 155
regeneration 62
regnum gratiae 127
regnum potentiae 127
renewal 17, 28, 98, 156
repentance 61, 73, 74, 79
revival, definition 17-18, essential characteristics 20-27
Riga 133
Roberts, Evan 133
Roberts, Maurice 130, 132
Roberts, Richard Owen 81
Roman Catholic Church 28, 87, 115
Roman Catholicism 115
Romania 134-136, 154
Rouen 90
Rowlands, Daniel 153
Russia 133
Ryland, John, Jr 97

S

sanctification 46, 90, 153
Sanhedrin 56
Satan 24, 30-32, 37, 43-45, 54, 56, 59, 61, 69, 74, 107, 129, 150, 158
Savanarola 87
Samuel 81, 85-86
Scotland 58, 77, 91, 95-97, 101, 112
Second Baptist Church 136
Second Coming 37
Second Great Awakening 91
Seminary, Fuller 31
Shekina glory 20

Some Thoughts Concerning the
*   Present Revival* 96
South Africa 13, 30, 93, 103,
    113
sovereign grace 63
sovereignty of God 62
Spain 105, 115
Spalatin, George 89
Spurgeon, C. H. 113, 133
Spurgeon, Thomas 133
Sri Lanka 13
Stephen 56, 64
Stewart, James 133
Still, William 112
Suffolk 29
Sutcliff, John 97, 99
Sweden 77
Switzerland 87

T

Taylor, Michael 113
Tear Fund 162
The Churchman 111
The Daily Telegraph 105, 134
The Great Awakening 25
The Korean Pentecost 138
The Mystery of Providence 41
The Next Forty Years for Christian
*   Missions* 134
The Presbyterian Magazine 10
The Religious Affections 24, 43,
    45
The Resurrection of the Chinese
*   Church* 134
Thessalonica 19
Thomas, Geoffrey 26
Thornwell, James Henley 11
Thoughts on Revival in New
    England 46
Toronto Blessing 31
Transformations 30

U

U. K., see Britain
Ulster 15, 25, 50
United Reformed Church 110,
    113

V

Van Staden, Hans 103
Van Zyl, Jim 155
Vermont 94
Victorian age 100
Vineyard Movement 31
Visiting, house-to-house 152
Von Amsdorf, Nicholas 89

W

Wagner, Peter 30, 31
Waldensians 87-88
Wales 19, 25, 30, 76, 78, 91,
    100-101, 109, 133, 153
Waldo, Peter 87
Warfield, B. B. 54
Watchmen 36-39
Weeping 64, 85, 101, 139
Welsh Revival 1904 19
Wesley, Charles 62
Wesley, John 99
Wesleyan Methodists 99, 102
Westminster Chapel 156
Whitefield, George 42, 100, 153,
    166, 169
William Fetler of Latvia 133
Wilson, James 107
Wimber, John 31
Wittenberg University 89
Wittenburg 89
Wycliffe 87, 186
Wycliffe Bible translators 19

Z

Zechariah 130
Zerubbabel 82, 130
Zion 21, 124, 129, 147
Zionist movements 20
Zwolle 88

A wide range of Christian books is available from Evangelical Press. If you would like a free catalogue please write to us or contact us by e-mail. Alternatively, you can view the whole catalogue online at our website:

www.evangelicalpress.org.

Evangelical Press
Faverdale North, Darlington, Co. Durham, DL3 0PH, England
e-mail: sales@evangelicalpress.org

Evangelical Press USA
P. O. Box 825, Webster, New York 14580, USA
e-mail: usa.sales@evangelicalpress.org